D1590091

Water Gardens & Natural Pools

Design & Construction

Peter Himmelhuber

4880 Lower Valley Road, Atglen, Pennsylvania 19310

Hartness Library System
Vermont Technical College
One Main Street
Randolph Center, VT 05061

Other Schiffer Books on Related Subjects

Creating Ponds, Brooks, and Pools: Water in the Garden. Ulrich Timm.
ISBN: 0764309153. $29.95
Designs for Garden Paths. Heidi Howcroft.
ISBN: 076430383X. $29.95
Landscape Design for Architectural Style: European Influenced. Scott Bradstreet.
ISBN: 9780764331060. $49.99
Landscape Design for Architectural Style: United States Original Styles. Scott Bradstreet.
ISBN: 9780764331077. $49.99
Outdoor Spaces in the Southwest. Damon Lang.
ISBN: 9780764332142. $39.99
Petite Patios & Intimate Garden Spaces. Keil Gisela Nik Barlo Jr. & Christa Brand.
ISBN: 0764320823. $19.95
Retreats to Retirement: Dream Homes to Reality. E. Ashley Rooney.
ISBN: 0764323393. $39.95
Sky Gardens. Signe Nielsen.
ISBN: 0764320041. $39.95
Victorian Gardens. Caroline Holmes.
ISBN: 0764318896. $29.95

Copyright © 2009 by Schiffer Publishing Ltd.
Previously published as Das Wassergarten-Baubuch by Callwey.
Library of Congress Control Number: 2009929632

All rights reserved. No part of this work may be reproduced or used in any form or by any means—graphic, electronic, or mechanical, including photocopying or information storage and retrieval systems—without written permission from the publisher.

The scanning, uploading and distribution of this book or any part thereof via the Internet or via any other means without the permission of the publisher is illegal and punishable by law. Please purchase only authorized editions and do not participate in or encourage the electronic piracy of copyrighted materials.

"Schiffer," "Schiffer Publishing Ltd. & Design," and the "Design of pen and ink well" are registered trademarks of Schiffer Publishing Ltd.

Designed by Ellen
Type set in Zurich BT/Zurich BT

ISBN: 978-0-7643-3367-5
Printed in China

Publication

All data were researched conscientiously and checked with great care. But no liability for changes or deviations can be accepted. At building sites and bodies of water in particular, there can be dangers, particularly for children. The premises should always be efficiently secured.

Schiffer Books are available at special discounts for bulk purchases for sales promotions or premiums. Special editions, including personalized covers, corporate imprints, and excerpts can be created in large quantities for special needs. For more information contact the publisher:

Published by Schiffer Publishing Ltd.
4880 Lower Valley Road
Atglen, PA 19310
Phone: (610) 593-1777; Fax: (610) 593-2002
E-mail: Info@schifferbooks.com

For the largest selection of fine reference books on this and related subjects, please visit our web site at:
www.schifferbooks.com
We are always looking for people to write books on new and related subjects. If you have an idea for a book please contact us at the above address.

This book may be purchased from the publisher.
Include $5.00 for shipping.
Please try your bookstore first.
You may write for a free catalog.

In Europe, Schiffer books are distributed by
Bushwood Books
6 Marksbury Ave.
Kew Gardens
Surrey TW9 4JF England
Phone: 44 (0) 20 8392 8585; Fax: 44 (0) 20 8392 9876
E-mail: info@bushwoodbooks.co.uk
Website: www.bushwoodbooks.co.uk

CONTENTS

Introduction

What Importance Does Water Have for People, Animals, and Plants?

It is the same with water as with so many other things: their value only becomes clear when they are lacking. While the lack of drinking water can have a life-threatening effect on people after just a few days, the lack of water in gardens becomes visible, especially in hot spells. Sensitive plants begin to shrivel after a few days without water. The value of water as a formative element also becomes evident if not enough of it is applied.

Gardens without bodies of water—in the form of springs, ponds or brooks— appear more lifeless than those with standing or spraying water. Not only are the plants dependent on it, but so are the animals. Soon after a body of water is created, thirsty songbirds arrive. Dragonflies come to the garden while the pond is being built, as if they knew that there would soon be water there. The watery element is unavoidable for animals that live in it. Fish, frogs, salamanders, and many insects only settle in a garden when they find water there. Fish and amphibians are even attached to their home. They can grow old if the conditions of life suit them. Of course, the body of water must be deep enough so that on cold winter days it does not freeze to the bottom. A protected environment is also needed, so that the animals are undisturbed or find resting places to withdraw into. Finally, tame animals like cats and dogs also have uses for the water.

WATER—SOURCE OF LIFE
Creating Generously

Food and Formative Element

Just like too little water, too much of it can be harmful. Floods after steady rainfall, brought on by the canalization and grading of rivers, result in damage to buildings.

It is all the more important to provide additional flood plain for watercourses. The reshaping of river and brook courses and the creation of flood plains has come to have a great significance in the process of shaping landscapes. Even in a garden, means of restraining water are possible. Some cisterns and rainwater collecting systems contribute to storing excessive rainwater. Large containers have capacities of several thousand liters. Seen overall, collecting rain in cisterns and rain barrels is very noticeable. It relieves the canalization and reduces the consumption of valuable drinking water by great numbers of people. This water can be used to water the garden.

Plants are attracted to the element of water. Typical water plants, like the yellow flag *(Iris pseudacorus)*, can survive only briefly without sufficient ground moisture. When they can grow lavishly, these long-lived shore plants form luxuriant stands that bloom reliably every year.

PREREQUISITES AND PLANNING
Bodies of Water in the Garden

Utilizing Formative Possibilities

On principle, it is advisable to plan a pond as large as possible, for a large pond looks better and is also more stable than a little puddle. Above all, it is advisable to plan different zones for shore, shallow-water and deep-water plants.

During excavation, plateaus are created at various levels, so that the plants can easily be planted there. Avoid steep slopes, for the gravel is washed off them and even the plants cannot hang on. Where steep slopes cannot be avoided, such as in swimming pools, one should plan, particularly in foil ponds, on building with hand-hewn natural stone, building walls of artificial stone, or attaching grids of wood laths. Otherwise the black synthetic material becomes visible later and is not protected from damage. The deepest place in the finished pond should be about 120 cm under ground level, so that the water cannot freeze all the way to the ground and the animals have an area to withdraw to. The bed of the pond must be dug out some 20 cm deeper for the sand cushion. Scarcely anyone builds a water garden "only" for animals or natural living space. Even an observer of nature will always design it so that it serves for learning as well as looking, and besides that, it should be more or less decorative. According to wishes and conceptions, though, water gardens develop in very different ways. Just like typical decorations, useful corners or living areas, water gardens can take on their very own character. There is never a purely decorative or purely useful garden, and every natural pond has a decorative value, and every decorative pond has a use. In a botanical garden, the pond serves mainly as a home for selected water plants—naturally this layout also has its charm for viewers and offers a home to many living creatures. A basin for decorative fish, in turn, is created according to other criteria, although it can also be valuable for plants and, not least, for people. And even a fountain in a garden can have varied uses, in that it provides a spray of water for show, gives birds drinking water, and necessary moisture to floating plants.

Bodies of Water in the Garden

Pond for Plants	Pond for Animals	Pond for People	Special Types
Exotic basin	Goldfish pond	Swimming pool	Brook
Water lily pond	Bird drinker	Paddling pool	Cascade
Floating plants and amphibians	Biotope for insects	Kneipp basin	Rainwater collector
Clear pool		Spray fountain	Water containers

In a Japanese garden, water is an essential formative element. The clever layout and arrangement of natural stones and plants makes extraordinary water gardens possible.

Legal Matters

Unfortunately, bodies of water in gardens are often the scenes of accidents that could have been avoided by safety measures. For this reasons there are legal requirements that contribute to the prevention of personal injury, avoidance of damage to structures or to neighborly peace. Thus ponds or swimming pools in private gardens are allowed only up to certain sizes. For example, according to Bavarian law, such bodies of water are allowed to have a maximum volume of only 100 cubic meters. Regulations concerning their use are also to be noted. Thus building a pond for small animals such as ducks or geese is sometimes not allowed. Here the building ordinances of the cities and communities take precedence over state laws. As a rule, keeping farm animals in new residential developments is forbidden. Before excavating a pond bed for raising ducks or fish, for example, the legal regulations dealing with construction should be checked. Information can also be had from the appropriate authorities. Even before digging one's own well, [p. 13] it is recommended that one obtain information from the responsible office. The water department will let you

know whether there are objections to a well for reasons of water conservation. Normally, though, well water may be used to water a garden. Only for household use is permission required, preceded by thorough tests. Often several offices must be consulted. The water department grants permission, if there are no objections on account of water hygiene, while the district council is responsible for permitting a private well for reasons of construction law, and the city or community government makes decisions, among others, as regards the construction regulations in a settlement. But this should not scare you away; usually building a pond requires no permission if it involves decorative ponds, small brooks or similar projects. Information avoids unpleasant surprises and gives assurance, for example, if the neighbors unexpectedly complain about the pond after it is finished or even in the course of building it. Naturally, the next-door neighbors should be informed for the sake of neighborhood peace, even if there is no legal objection. Perhaps even border-crossing projects can be done in cooperation. Likewise, consideration for the occupants of your own house is advisable, such as in a multifamily house with rented apartments. A pond may have to be ruled out to protect small children or handicapped residents.

* **First be informed, then build**
The building regulations of the individual German states can be obtained in paperback at bookstores.

Requirements, Location, Situation

Sunny or Shady

A body of water should be a permanent part of a garden. Planning errors are thus to be avoided from the start. And here the rule is: The larger the pond, the more permanent its biological system. By nature, every body of water is constantly subjected to changes in weather and growth. A pond—like a garden—is never finished. But the basis must make sense.

So note a few ground rules:

▶ The more volume, the more constant the water remains, and the fewer changes a pond is exposed to.

▶ The sunnier the location, the greater the warming and thus the algae formation.

▶ The shadier the location, the less plant development—except for typical shade plants.

▶ The more inaccessible the water garden is, the more safely fauna and flora can develop.

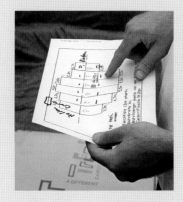

When the location, size, and shape are determined, a plan for ordering pond foil can be finalized.

In a sunny location the water plants form luxuriant growths, but they are easy to reduce.

Also applicable:

▶ Nutritious soil favors algae formation and clouding of the water.

▶ Water plants are effective water filters.

▶ Water plants are self-sufficient and not dependent on nutritious soil or fertilizer.

▶ Water plants also produce waste and rotting products—the more plants, the more humus forms on the bottom.

In a full-sun location, the warm water provides the best growth conditions for algae, as long as they do not yet have any competition there from water plants.

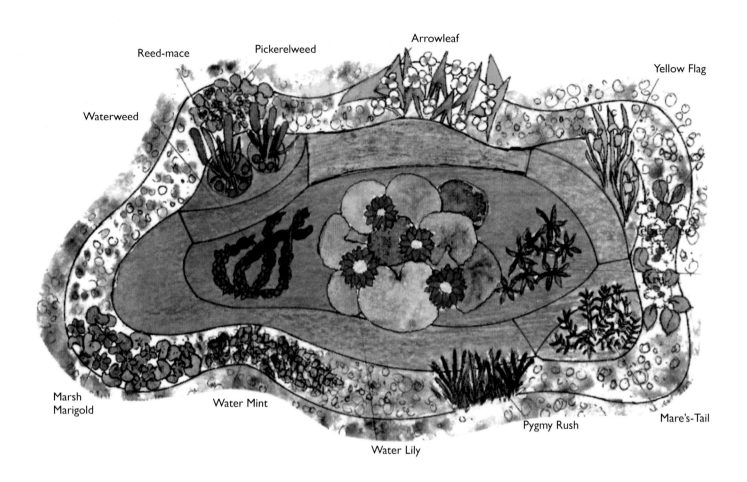

Reed-mace

Pickerelweed

Arrowleaf

Yellow Flag

Waterweed

Marsh
Marigold

Water Mint

Pygmy Rush

Mare's-Tail

Water Lily

Even a small pond basin, here a plastic basin with preformed plant buckets, offers abundant space for several chosen types. It is always recommended to plant several plants of a species in groups. Such tuffets develop later, when they form thick growths.

Size, Format, and Profile

The size of a body of water depends primarily on the size of the plot of ground and the usable area for this formative element. Usually there should be, along with a pond in a garden, enough room for a lawn, vegetable beds, a border of shrubs, for lines of trees, and other elements. Depending on use and preference for water in a garden, the lawns and beds are kept small in favor of a large pond layout. If they are omitted completely, the entire garden area can be laid out as a pond. Then the water garden begins right at the terrace and extends to the boundary fence. Such a large wet zone offers many formative possibilities. For example, if an area of 300 to 500 square meters, otherwise available for an ordinary garden, is planned for a pond, a manifold garden formation is possible. Along with different water zones, such as damp, shallow-water, and deep-water zones, even islands are created, in that during excavation hills are left here

Weinlaube — Marhise — Zaun + Schuppen — Brunnen — Rasen-pflaster — Rasen — "Stein" garten — Teich — Obst- + Blütenhecke — Rasen — Gemüsebeete — Kompost

and there, or sand-hills are piled up in the pond bed in the construction process. Later, after planting, such islands form ideal resting places for songbirds. Naturally, the creation of islands—especially in ponds that are not planned to be large—requires a sufficient area. In small ponds, the building of islands where the water depth is at least 70 cm. is otherwise attainable only with steep walls. Instead of integrating fixed islands made of sand-hills or by digging out soil, floating islands can also be created in any pond

later. Pontoons of plastic or wood serve as a base that can be planted and livened with plant substrata.

Pond foils make any desired shape and profile possible. The elastic plastic material fits any pond bed. The shape of the body of water thus depends more on the garden terrain than the material—provided a hard plastic basin is preferred to the foil. Then the shape and profile are determined by the choice of a certain product. On the other hand, the pond

Paper is patient—before finished things are created in the garden, it pays to play with ideas in simple sketches. The designs can be changed as you please or be discussed with specialists. This preliminary design also represents the example in the swimming-pool chapter.

foil allows round or straight shapes. Thus the pond can border directly on the pavement of a terrace, while the shore on the garden side can curve into the lawn. Similarly, existing trees or beds can be bordered in any desired shape. The value of the elastic foil becomes particularly noticeable in the shaping of pond combinations. Thus it is possible to cover steep walls in swimming areas while the plant zones are flat. Just as with foil, pond fleece fits any profile.

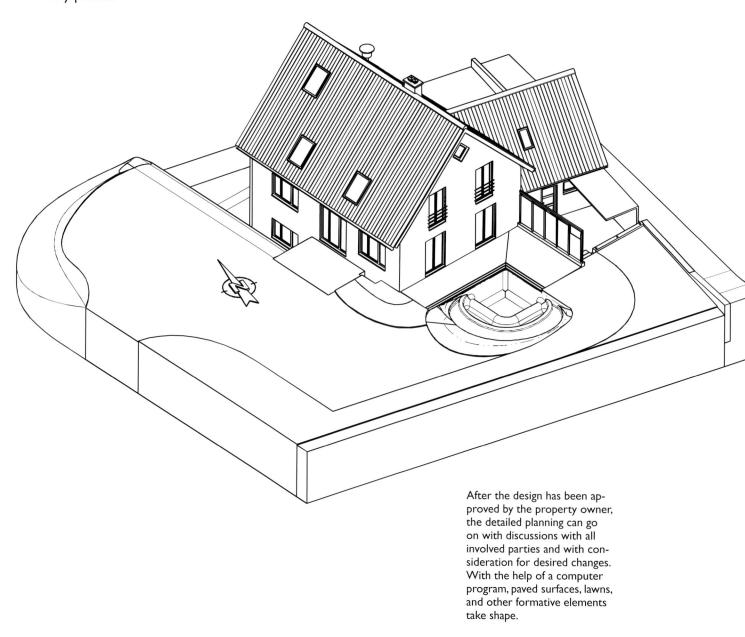

After the design has been approved by the property owner, the detailed planning can go on with discussions with all involved parties and with consideration for desired changes. With the help of a computer program, paved surfaces, lawns, and other formative elements take shape.

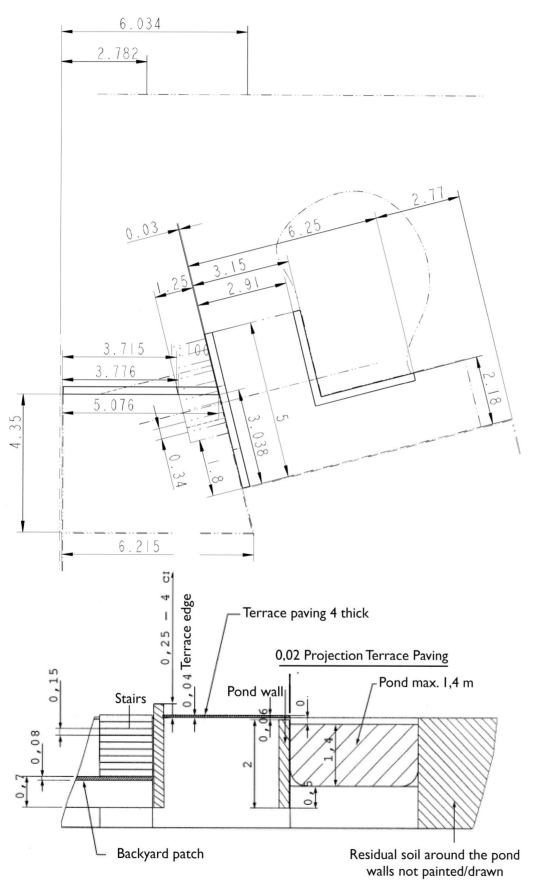

6.034
2.782
0.03
2.77
6.25
3.15
1.25
2.91
3.715
1.00
3.776
5.076
2.18
4.35
0.34
1.8
3.038
5
6.215

Exact measurements are necessary during the whole construction phase. Thus the quantities of materials, such as concrete and structural steel for the supporting walls, and the parts needed for the basins, can be calculated exactly. The drawing shows the pond layout as seen from the house. The work steps are depicted in phase photos in the "Building a Swimming Pool" chapter. On the basis of the drawing, the shovel driver can also be well informed. A detailed plan and, if necessary, a discussion with architects or planners, is valuable, especially with difficult ground conditions or an unfavorable location, such as on a slope. Thus resulting damage, such as from insufficient support walls, can be avoided.

0,25 – 4 cm
0,04 Terrace edge
Terrace paving 4 thick
0,02 Projection Terrace Paving
Pond max. 1,4 m
0,15
Stairs
Pond wall
0,06
0,08
2
1,4
0,7

Backyard patch

Residual soil around the pond walls not painted/drawn

19

Park Gardens and Displays

Before deciding on a pond, it is a good idea to evaluate already existing bodies of water. Old overgrown sites or even new ponds are often found in communal model gardens, in displays of pond-building or landscaping businesses, in botanical gardens or parks in the neighborhood. Spend some time by the water and the effect of this special element becomes tangible. Catalogs also make it possible to select particular plants. Information about plants, animals, or details of bodies of water, such as depth, costs, care, etc., can be obtained from the owners. They will surely also indicate problems, such as with water quality, algae or unwanted pond visitors. In addition, technical elements, such as pumps, filters or ducting are

While typical foil ponds can be formed freely without plans, exact plans are needed for large ponds or very symmetrical bodies of water. Above all, when specialist firms require specifications, such as for a stainless steel fountain pillar or a Kneipp basin, or measurements for concrete or natural stone constructions are needed, scale drawings are indispensable.

explained, especially for grounds with spring stones, brooks or cascades. This information avoids planning errors and eases the decision for a particular type of pond, for an intended material or selected plants, or it inspires one to make changes in the original building plans. It is good to know how long the water gardens have existed, and whether they functioned properly over that time. Above all, before one decides on expensive construction—like that of a swimming pool—viewing existing projects is recommended. The best advertisement for a pond-building firm is the satisfaction of the owners with their layout and their recommendation of that firm. To be sure, cost estimates should be obtained from several firms. Several offers make price and performance comparisons possible.

Building Materials

Materials for the Water Garden

On a walk through a well-stocked building-material shop or the display area of a garden-building firm, one is offered a good opportunity to select materials for one's own projects. Along with a row of industrial materials made of concrete—such as well rings in many sizes, plastic shaping pieces in varying shapes, or wooden elements in diverse versions—there are all kinds of natural stones, cinder blocks or natural stone slabs ready to buy or to be worked into finished projects. Help can also be had from the catalogs of dealers and producers. It is worthwhile to visit several displays and request catalogs at the right time before planning a water-garden project. In particular, catalogs of specialist manufacturers of pond-building materials and accessories should be obtained; they also allow price comparisons. A valuable source of information is the Internet, where pond foil, pumps, filters, and many other products can be sought. "Surfing" in this medium is rewarding, not only in choosing materials and technical products, but also regarding special questions about water gardens, or problems with algae, unknown insects, and the like.

MATERIALS AND TECHNIQUES
Beginning with Excavation

Left: Lime soil is suitable for the basin of a pond if it is compacted with a vibration compactor. Of course water always seeps through the walls.

Above: The boulders that are exposed during excavation can be used as materials for a dry wall or a rock garden by the pond. Only the excavator can move big boulders.

Various Soils

In nature, bodies of water are formed in low areas, especially in thick clay or lime beds. If such beds are at hand in the garden, the material for a watertight basin is already available.

Of course these soils are uncommon in typical home gardens, especially if the thick subsoil is dug out with an excavator and transported away by truck. Later, after the house is built, the building contractor replaces the removed soil with good garden topsoil. As a rule, this consists of sandy loam or loamy sand with a portion of humus, which is usually obtained in the process of building new residential areas on formerly agricultural land. But a "well-developed" clay or lime soil can be retained if it appears during excavation and is wanted as material for a body of water. Depending on the composition and thickness of the layer, the clay and lime soil is more or less watertight. This is already evident after a heavy rain. Usually the water trickles through present capillary tubes, dead roots or other ingredients into the underground. Then the clay or lime soil only needs an added covering, perhaps of pure clay without additives, or working with a vibrator or tamper, to be usable as a watertight pond basin—or the body of water may serve as a swamp basin, which can dry out at times or always be filled, perhaps with rainwater from the roof of the house. Building a pond with purchased clay from a pit is expensive and laborious compared with building a pond with foil. After the heavy clumps of clay are delivered, they must be worked promptly so they do not dry out and harden.

Pumps, Filters, and Such

Along with the pond basin, which can consist of clay, concrete or plastic depending on its type, and the covering of gravel, sand or other natural materials, only selected water plants are needed for a typical pond. If the pond is built properly, it needs no special filter technology. Yet technical devices can be very useful. For example, with the help of a special solar pump and the modules that go with it, a water fountain can be created. If the water garden is meant to be a home for many fish, especially big koi fish, then installing a capable filter must not be neglected. Special systems can be had in the trade and installed in the water or on the shore. The capability depends on the volume of water and the degree of pollution. Most filters can be removed if one sees that they do not accomplish the filtering when in operation. A pump is also needed for the operation of a brook flow. Here the capability depends on the desired flow and the required height of the water and diameter of the duct.

To pump your water out of a cistern or well, typical immersion pumps suffice. So-called jet pumps that stand in a dry place and take in well or rainwater have also proved themselves. In combination with a pressure regulator, such pumps are available as household water instruments. To operate a pump, an electric connection must be available. In the process of building the pond, a ground cable for it must be laid. Electric plugs by the pond allow, among other things, the use of lights, and are available for running electric devices such as pond cleaning or water-removal pumps.

PLASTICS

Foils and Fleeces

Dependable Foils

For some years, garden ponds have been the points of interest in many gardens. Special pond foils make their construction simpler. They are reasonably priced, easy to work, and yet stable.

Although the foils are made of plastic, one can use them for a nearly natural pond—provided that you lay out the good piece correctly, so that nothing more of it is seen later, after the pond is set up.

If you follow all the rules, a luxuriant biotope with a natural character can develop, scarcely to be distinguished from a natural pond. In any case, it is not important to plants or animals whether the pond was laid out artificially or created by nature. For example, the first dragonflies and songbirds often come to drink during construction.

The most useful material for pond building is foil, for it can be worked without special experience and means, is elastic, 100% watertight, and costs relatively little. This stands out particularly during construction. This special pond foil fits the created bed precisely. It makes any desired shape possible. Stiff plastic basins are much harder to install and produce certain pond shapes. Unfortunately, this universal pond basin also has a few disadvantages. First, the plastic has to be produced laboriously. The compounds that result sometimes contain elements (like cadmium and chlorine in PVC foils) that can be poisonous if they, for example, are released through the rotting of the foil. Although many manufacturers give a ten-year guarantee, every foil decomposes slowly. It is especially annoying if repairs to a really misshapen foil become necessary. Of course you can decisively influence the durability by buying a high-quality brand and working it properly. So do not economize in the wrong place, and work carefully when you decide for a foil pond. Meanwhile, there are grown-in foil ponds that are more than twenty years old and show no thin spots.

Pond basins are available with sandy edges. The natural material is melted firmly into the plastic. In the same way, sand- or gravel-coated foils can be had. These special products are considerably more expensive than customary products.

Various Materials

Make sure that the foil is resistant to light and degradation. Earlier polyethylene foils (such as household foils and plastic covers) are fully unsuitable; they are, of course, environment-friendly, but in time they become brittle and crack. Special pond foils made of polyethylene (PE), so-called eco-pond foils, are ideal. They are extremely durable and yet environment-friendly. Pond foils made of PVC (polyvinyl chloride) contain softeners and stabilizers, which protect particularly against damage by ultra-violet rays. They also contain chlorine, which escapes from the ashes when burned and has a poisonous effect. PE pond foils are thus preferable to PVC foils in every case. Some manufacturers also offer rubber foils. This natural-based material also has good and bad qualities. Rubber foils are just as durable and stress-resistant as synthetic plastic foils. But the raw material must be obtained and transported at just as much expense. In addition, additives like softeners and stabilizers must be added during foil production. Along with black foils, brown and green ones are also available. But the color is not important, since the foil is covered anyway with gravel, sand or subsoil. Foils coated with sand or gravel are also available in the trade. Their use is a matter of taste.

The stability of pond foil can be recognized at a touch. GFK basins are recognizable by their rigid edges. Simple PP or PE basins give under pressure and twist.

Various Strengths

Pond foils exist in 0.5, 1, and 1.5-mm thicknesses. Foils 1 mm thick have proven themselves. They are easy to work and yet sufficiently tear-resistant and root-resistant. Direct danger from root damage is only a threat from nearby trees. But these usually seek the simplest route and pass by the foil instead of penetrating it. Of course they press on the foil, but the elastic material gives to a certain degree without tearing.

Pond foils can be shaped as desired, which makes them valuable for covering complex shapes. To protect the elastic plastic sheets, special pond fleeces can be had to spread on the pond bed.

When you spread out the pond foil, avoid tension. Folds, on the other hand, do no harm. Later they disappear under the layer of gravel and offer hiding places to the pond creatures. So that enough substance in available to cover critical spots, the foil should be bought larger than needed.

Pond fleeces can be had in various types as yard goods. They are pollution-free acrylic materials that are fully rot-resistant. The color is unimportant. White products are suitable, as are bluish ones. When the very light fleeces are laid out, weighting them with gravel avoids them being blown off.

Protection for the Foil

Yet you should prepare the pond bed very carefully with foil. It is especially important to remove thick roots and dig out or pad pointed objects. The work is worth doing, for a padded pond bed lengthens the life span of the foil markedly. Not only can pointed stones or rubble endanger the foil, but so can other materials; artificial materials in particular can make holes. Adhesives, thickening bands, tar paper, and the like grasp the pond foil and cause wear at the contact points. Strengthen or attack the foil only with recommended aids. Also avoid contact between foil and impregnated wood. If you, for example, want to cover a wooden pond made of railroad ties with foil, you should separate the two materials with fleece or some other protective matting.

Buy Bigger Than You Need

After excavation, it is best to buy the foil as one complete piece, for the builders have more experience in attaching individual pieces. You can also order special dimensions. It is important that you buy the foil bigger than you need. It must project at the shore so as to be pressed firmly into the pond bed and sag under water pressure.

Disposing of Excess

Never burn foil or foil containers in the furnace. The designation "residue-free when burned" applies only to special trash burners! Scraps or old foil therefore should go to recycling depots. Scraps of pond foil are also suitable for mulching flowerbeds. One can still get rid of them after use.

Padding and Substructure

Every pond basin is only as enduring as its protection. For this reason it is important to pad the pond bottom after excavation if the bottom does not consist of sand, loam or another fine-grained mineral substratum. The pond basin should never be applied directly to soil with humus or roots, for the humus structure is changed in time by numerous ground life forms and organic ingredients. For example, hollow spots can form when roots die off and give way sooner or later to the pressure of the pond basin. The pressure can eventually cause cracks. Stony soil is just as unsuitable under the pond basin, for the stones press permanently on the walls. This is especially true in case of frost, which reaches a depth of some 70 cm and pushes the stones up. In time the pond basin becomes weakened by the constant tension. It is simplest to prepare a suitable substructure on a sand or loam ground.

After excavation, you need only remove stones, roots, and other coarse items. After smoothing the uneven spots, the pond bed is ready to be covered. If the ground is full of roots or stones, removing them is hardly worth your while. You should dig out the pond bed some 20 cm deeper than planned and cover it with an equally thick layer of sand. Thick roots of living trees may need to be removed if they intrude into the pond bed. This is best done with a saw after the roots have been exposed as much as possible. This additional work is a nuisance, but it avoids repairs later, for every pond basin lies properly on a pad of sand.

Fleeces

Instead of sand, the trade also offers special pond-protecting matting. These non-degradable fleece mats made of plastic were developed especially for use under pond foil. They can scarcely be penetrated, even by sharp stones, and thus give the pond foil optimal protection from below. Because of their light weight, they can also be moved easily, such as to a steep slope where a layer of sand would scarcely stay. To be sure, pond-protective matting made of fleece has its price; a square meter of fleece costs as much as a square meter of low-priced pond foil. So check even before building the pond whether the ground at the chosen site is in order. If not, perhaps another site can be found.

If you build your pond on a slope, it is important to secure the grade. The back of a slope may need to be supported by a wall or palisade in case a steep slope is created by excavation. The pond must also be supported at the front of the slope if you have dumped excavated soil there. This may be possible by building a massive dry wall.

Working with Pond Foils

Pond foil is a popular material, not only because of its light weight, availability, and elasticity, but also because it is easy to work. You can bend, cut, and glue foil. The folds that are formed in the pond bed do no harm. They offer hiding places for small creatures and disappear from sight under the gravel or sand layer when the pond bottom is covered. Of course, working it calls for special attention, for small mistakes can have long-lasting results. So buy only well-made name brands with long-life guarantees. Usually materials in typical sizes are sold from the roll. In buying by the meter or yard, you must almost always accept a cut. But you can also order your foil in the size you want. When installing a large pond, this also has the advantage of not having to glue the joints yourself. Most manufacturers give their usual guarantee for seamed material made to meet individual needs. If you piece your pond foil yourself, this guarantee is ruled out; at least for the seams. Avoid making seams yourself, for they are always weak points. But if they are necessary (as in brook beds), proceed carefully. There are also various means and possibilities—from special adhesives to adhesive tapes from a roll, attachable with hot air. In all work with foil, a suitable bottom and "appropriate" clothing such as sneakers are important to avoid minor damage.

HARD PLASTIC
Rigid Basins

Readymade Shapes

If the body of water is to serve as a wading pool, a hard plastic basin may under some conditions be better suited for it. Besides, small plastic basins can also be used for water gardens on balconies and terraces.

Every garden center offers such basins in various sizes, shapes, and qualities. The simplest types are round or rectangular plaster basins. Such plastic containers made of PP (Polypropylene) or PE (Polyethylene) are suitable for mini-ponds on terraces by being disguised with wood, or as birdbaths sunk invisibly into the ground in a garden. For more water volume and surface there are special pond basins made of PE or GFK (glass-fiber reinforced polyester). PE basins can be had in sizes to some 2 meters in diameter and 50-cm depth, in various shapes with integrated shallow water zones, or with smooth steep walls.

Such pond basins are sufficiently stable when they are sunk in the ground without being twisted. Stress, such as from unevenness in the ground during installation, can cause cracks if PE basins do not have reinforced walls.

* Protecting Animals
Plastic basins with steep walls are especially dangerous for woodchucks. The animals come to the basin to drink and fall into the water. So they can easily reach the water and their way back to the shore is not blocked, the steep walls should be sloped, for example, with gravel or sand.

When you make a choice, it pays to check the various pool basins closely. The difference between light PE basins and GKF basins can be recognized at a touch. GFK basins feature extreme stiffness and stability under pressure. The layers of fiberglass weave are also visible. Such basins are produced by a spray-fiber process and partially in several layers—as in boat building—by hand-applied process. For such basins, there is a manufacturer's guarantee of fifteen years. Usually, though, they last for many decades. Along with complete basins in round, oval or angular formats, some manufacturers also offer elements that can be combined systematically. Thus hard plastic ponds of any size, suitable for stable swimming pools, can be made. The parts have to be ordered according to plan. After they are delivered and set in the ground, screws create firm joints. Besides pond elements, there are special bath-building elements of hard plastic, with smooth surfaces or sanded inner walls.

While simple polyester basins must be set firmly in the ground so as to stand the water pressure, rigid GFK basins are also suitable for free standing on the ground surface. Thus high ponds that, for example, have a place on a large terrace, or serve as swimming pools in gardens, can be made. The black plastic walls can be covered with wood or dry walls of natural stone.

Unlike foils, rigid plastic basins do not fit the ground; they are, so to speak, independent and need a well-prepared location. After being placed in the pond bed, a level helps to set them horizontally. As soon as the pond basin is sitting right, it can be built in. Flooding it with water holds the basin in the desired position.

Deep pond basins are dangerous places in a garden. To protect small children, filling with gravel is helpful. After pre-filling, the body of water serves as a wading pool. Later, when the children are no longer in danger, the gravel can be removed and used to form the border.

BUILDING WITH CONCRETE
Using Readymade Shaped Parts

An alternative to plastics is concrete. There are, for example, concrete rings (shaft or well rings) in varying sizes, which are very useful for building a well or cistern. Naturally, one can also use these rings in other ways, such as in building a garden pond.

Selection

Concrete rings can be had in various sizes in the building trade, or directly from concrete works. For pond building, large-diameter rings 50 cm high can be used. Depending on the desired pond size, they can be rings 100, 150 or 200 cm in diameter. The prices of these industrial materials are quite reasonable. A concrete ring with 100-cm diameter and 50-cm height costs about 100 Euro. Of course the transport costs are added. The building-material dealers can supply information (see the yellow pages). The rings can also be examined and chosen before ordering.

Delivery

The rings are delivered by a crane truck and unloaded directly onto the building site. The location has to be prepared properly for them, since moving them on your own is possible only for short distances, if at all. The rings can, of course, be rolled when they are standing upright, but this means of moving them is not recommended. Uneven ground or motion can make the rings crack or break. Naturally, rolling is also dangerous. The crane truck sets the rings down right on the desired spot. The excavation for the concrete pond has to be prepared already, or the site must be leveled if the body of water is not to be sunk into the ground.

Placing

A concrete ring, like any other water container, can be located in various places in a garden. It can be a location on a terrace or off in an unused corner of the garden. The situation naturally derives from the plant growth and microclimate. In a sunny situation, different water and shore plants thrive than in a shady place. This should be considered in selecting a location. Naturally, the site has to be reachable by the truck. A special substructure is normally not important. The rings can be set directly on the ground. The site must, though, have been leveled before the ring is unloaded. This is done with the help of a level and lath. If the ring is to set firmly into the ground, an appropriately deep ditch has to be dug out. The excavated soil can be used to form the shore after the ring is in place.

Formation

If a deep pond or a rainwater cistern is to be made, several rings can be set one on another. Several such bodies of water arranged in groups look really nice. One of these concrete basins could be filled only with gravel, another with water plants, and a third could be a spring. The gray concrete walls disappear into the ground when the bodies of water are sunk completely. They may also be made brighter with façade paint or natural stones. Surrounding them with luxuriant green plants is also possible.

Sealing

The concrete rings need no special covering. They are also watertight without foil if the ground is sealed with concrete. A sufficient quantity of fresh concrete is needed for this. In all, the concrete bottom should be some 10 cm thick. Mixing small quantities of concrete can be done by hand in a basin with a trowel or shovel. To prepare greater quantities, an electric concrete mixer is needed. To produce the tough concrete, gravel, cement and water are needed. To four parts of gravel, add one part of cement and some water for stirring. The fresh concrete is smoothed with a trowel after being poured into the ring. Setting takes about twenty-four hours. Several days go by before the concrete bottom is fully hardened. Painting with watertight material makes the joint fully sealed. This gray cement brew can be painted, which seals the rough pores of the raw concrete surface. After drying, the pond basin can finally be arranged and flooded.

Arranging and Planting

Any possible water plants can be used as greenery. The concrete ring always offers a water depth of 50 cm. Soil as nutrient-poor as possible can be put in. Excavated sandy soil is suitable. Loamy garden soil can be thinned with sand. Nutrient-rich humus should not be used. It is sufficient to put substrata in the concrete ring only where the plants will go. After putting in the chosen plants, covering the ground with gravel prevents particles of soil from floating away. Strewing with gravel also makes it look decorative. Right after planting, flooding can be done. After filling, the water is still milky and dull—which clears up in a few days.

Animals Come on Their Own

Like any body of water, a concrete-ring pond is also a valuable source of life for many animals. Birds come to drink and bathe. Dragonflies and other insects also come on their own. If woodchucks, mice or other four-legged creatures have access to the pond, especially when it is even with ground level, they should be able to get back onto the shore. In steep places, which a concrete-ring pond naturally has, passages can be made of gravel or natural stones.

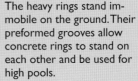
The heavy rings stand immobile on the ground. Their preformed grooves allow concrete rings to stand on each other and be used for high pools.

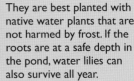
They are best planted with native water plants that are not harmed by frost. If the roots are at a safe depth in the pond, water lilies can also survive all year.

Fresh concrete can be used in any shapes. With the help of the appropriate shapes, large round concrete basins can be formed.

NATURAL BUILDING MATERIALS
Using Wood

Manifold Possibilities

Wood, the natural material, has a special value in building water gardens, both for shaping bodies of water and for formation and fencing. Massive timbers can form a stable enclosure for a high pond and then allow a watertight covering with foil.

Wooden planks are useful for building wooden terraces, wooden steps, and bridges on the pond. Piers of concrete form strong bases for them. Nice massive structures are made of wooden boards that are attached to the planks with stainless steel screws. Planks, boards, and beams of larch, locust or Douglas fir have proved themselves as garden building materials by water. Whoever prefers exotic woods, such as the dark brown Bangkirai from Indonesia, should choose ecologically unproblematic goods (tropical woods from documentable commercial forest plantations).

Constructive Wood Protection

Garden wood is always exposed to the weather. Wetness, wind, and sunlight affect the surface. The wood turns gray in time and starts to crack. Rotting is speeded up by wood fungi through contact with the soil. Bad spots also result from standing rainwater. Constructive wood protection helps to counteract this. Covering boards on the tops of posts prevent moisture from penetrating. In the same way, bottom boards on wooden decks are handy to prevent moisture from remaining by providing small spaces between them. In principle, an airy condition with sufficient distance from the ground lengthens the life of all wooden structures.

Willow Wickerwork

Living Structures

Here are many uses and places for wickerwork in the garden. From the long, elastic withes you can make protective fences, slope holders, climbing helpers, containers for water plants, natural trellises, and many other formative elements. Thick trunks or branches serve as fence posts, palisades to secure slopes, wood for building bridges, steps, and the like. The special feature of it is that living willow wood also remains durable without impregnation. The trunks and stalks grow roots where they touch the ground and grow into the building site.

Willow withes that are cut during their growing time break easily and are useless for wickerwork. The right time to cut willow withes is therefore in the winter season. When sap is not running, the trees and shrubs allow cutting back old branches. This radical intervention even arouses them to grow and develop strong new shoots. Naturally, simply cutting down any willow trees anywhere in the world of nature is not allowed. For good cutting, use either individual willows that grow in a garden or such examples as, for example, are blown down by autumn storms or are pruned on purpose. Willows were formerly grown along brooks and drainage ditches specifically as sources of raw materials. The trees were cut back radically to the trunk every year. Thus the typical pollard willows developed in time. The meter-long yearly growth was used for basket weaving and other handicrafts. The long, elastic shoots of the basket willow *(Salix viminalis)* characterized by yellow bark were especially useful. But other species also develop useful material that finds uses today as before.

Willow wickerwork can be used in pond building to hold slopes of loose soil, especially piled-up heaps of it. While the shoots, driven vertically into the ground, form roots and spread, the horizontally woven-in withes hold the loose earth.

Above: In forestry schools, many trees and shrubs are grown from cuttings. Young shoots of cutting length are stuck into the ground in rows. They grow and form strong young plants. But willow shoots can also be encouraged to grow roots in a glass of water.

Upper right: The vital willow is even able to grow roots out of thick trunks. This growing power can be used deliberately in the garden. The butts are pointed and driven into the ground. They can serve as posts that give stability to the willow withes.

Right: Individual butts or even thick trunks that are rammed into the ground standing free can be grown as pollard willows. The young shoots are cut back strongly every year, so that increasingly bushy "heads" develop.

Growing Your Own Mother Plants

This unusual building material can be bought in special nurseries. It can also be acquired by yourself. Just a few withes obtained from healthy mother plants are enough for your first attempts. Old trees or bushy shrubs do not object to cutting a few shoots. From three or four shoots, small borders along the pond can be woven or climbing aids for plants at the water's edge can be formed. In any case, they suffice for the first attempts with this natural material. Small lengths of them can be used to increase some cut plants—about shear-length willow shoots form roots in the water. The rooted stuck-in shoots then grow in pots or garden beds and develop in their own way into strong trees or small bushes. Such types as grow long yearly shoots are the best sources of cuttings. They can be basket willow or white willow *(Salix alba)*, pussy willow *(S. caprea)*, or hoop willow *(S. daphnoides)*.

All kinds of willows grow best in constantly damp or water-bearing soils. From a formative standpoint, locations on natural waterways or an artistic garden pond are also ideal. Because of their tremendous vitality, willows are used infrequently as garden trees. Only in large gardens does a weeping willow sometimes stand, catching the eye with its long, drooping branches. In typical gardens, the hanging pussy willow *(Salix caprea* "Pendula") is planted more often, but it is scarcely used for cutting purposes. Of course some branches from the small trees can be had as decorative objects. The hanging pussy willows are also pruned only after they bloom in the spring. Then during the whole summer they keep putting out new flowering branches for the next year. If they were cut in the winter, the flowers would be lost along with the cuttings. The blossom time of white and sallow willows is also in the spring. They must be cut in the winter, though, for after blossoming their branches break.

They are then unsuitable for wickerwork. As for willows, there are also two types of plants; there are masculine and feminine types. Only the masculine produce the lovely bushy cattail blossoms. The feminine flowers are greenish and attract less attention. After pollination they form a richness of fine seeds that the wind distributes far into the environment. In this way these typical meadow trees move into the garden. There they are rarely wanted, as they grow quickly and strongly and overwhelm other plants. But willow saplings that have grown by themselves in a garden can be used as sources of cuttings.

Obtaining Cuttings

The strong young shoots that have grown in the past year are especially suited for wickerwork. These shoots can be several meters long. Above all, if the cutting plants are trimmed radically every year, they put out unusually long shoots. Cutting is possible from autumn, after the leaves fall, to just before the beginning of new growth in the following spring. To protect the mother plants, cutting should be done late in the winter, such as from January to February. Then the cuts heal better than after cutting in the autumn. In general, though, willows can bear cutting very well. They must often suffer wounds from nature, since the old wood becomes very brittle. In particular, the branches easily grow from the cutting places.

Sharp shears are needed for cutting. They make the work easier and protect the mother plants by leaving smooth cutting places that heal quickly. When cutting, make sure that disturbing and very thickly growing shoots are removed. Thus the cutting also helps to keep the willows healthy—in any case, trees that grow close to nature should be preserved. As for pollard willows that need a radical cutting of all new yearly shoots, only short stumps with a few buds remain.

Storing and Working

The cut withes are bundled and stored cool and dark until working. If a living fence is wanted, a quick evaluation is advised. The withes dry out during long storage. Then they are no longer able to grow. Willow withes that are intended for wreaths or other objects can also be stored longer; the young shoots remain very elastic. If necessary, soaking in water makes them flexible again.

Making Willow Fences

For a willow fence, one needs both the long withes used for weaving and some thicker branches or twigs. The number depends on the length of the fence and the intervals of the posts. In any case, the withes should not span too great a distance, so they will stay stiff between the posts. The posts have a firm grip if they are some 50 cm deep in the ground. They can be driven in with a hammer after being pointed. Splintered wood can be trimmed off later, so that the posts have smooth heads. In this way too, pollard willows are raised in big forestry schools. Their thick branches or trunks are simply driven into the ground and left to grow. After driving in the willow posts comes the weaving of the fence blocks. From the ground up, the young elastic withes are woven in, always in alternating directions, among three or more posts, depending on their lengths. But there is no strict pattern. It is important that the withes remain firm and form a stable woven material. In moist ground the fence posts grow roots. They often sprout in the following spring. Strong young shoots are usable as cuttings for woven work the next winter. Willow withes are also very suitable for natural fences and enclosures, as well as for gateway arches, and if they are long enough, for sitting places beside the water, climbing aids, and much more.

MINERAL BUILDING MATERIALS
Sand, Gravel, and Stone

Rounded Stones

The covering gravel comes from the local region. Ordinary rounded gravel also used in house building to level the ground is sufficient. Instead of, or along with, the gravel, sand can also be used. Sand is also the ideal material for curbing the foil. Before covering, it is spread out thickly enough in the pond bed.

Gravel is usually found in river valleys in thick beds under a covering of humus. The excavating companies lease the ground from its owners for excavation and get a permit from the responsible authorities. After the humus layer is removed, the gravel is accessible for excavation. It is then used as building material, especially in producing concrete and garden formation. Depending on the region, gravel can be produced by various means. The gravel originating from mountainous areas was originally transported to the lowlands by rivers in the form of broken pieces of rock. On the long trip down the river, this rock took on gravel's usual rounded form through the power of the rushing water and constant mutual friction. Ordinary river gravel can be had in various grain sizes directly from the quarries or from dealers. It consists of vari-

Depending on the region, the material for dry walls, rock gardens, and the like is often found just under the surface in mountainous regions. When the pit is dug out, the excavator brings the boulders to light that can be used there in the garden. Limestone, granite, or other types of rock, depending on the region, can also be had from a quarry or a stone company.

ous types of stone, as the rivers carry material to the valley from various mountain areas. For instance, Danube gravel is different from Upper Rhine gravel. This is also true of gravel from pits where it was already deposited in the Ice Age, When a certain gravel—say, with mainly white stones, or insignificant gray gravel—is wanted, this has to be pointed out when ordering it from the quarry or dealer. The size of the gravel depends on the sieve position. The raw gravel is worked in shaking sieves in the quarry. Thus in addition to unsorted gravel, which consists of stones of various sizes and is usually used for making concrete, special types of gravel can also be had. For example, a small-grained gravel with sizes from 12 to 22 mm is suitable for a Kneipp basin in a garden, since it is pleasant to step on. On the other hand, typical gravel with a grain of 32 to 40 mm is better used for shore formation.

Many Materials

Along with quarried stone, found pieces and fieldstone, many other stone types are suitable for garden formation. Along with the gravel used for building ponds and their surroundings, many other natural stone types have proved themselves. Natural stones form enduring additions by the water, such as paths. That is also true of small-stone pavement that is laid on a massive substructure of crushed stone. Large building material centers, paving companies or special natural stone dealers offer extensive assortments of various natural stone materials that can be seen in their displays. When making a choice, a price list is handy. A preliminary choice can be made at home with the help of a building material catalog. Advice for using natural stone can often be obtained at regional garden shows or in public gardens.

Sand is indispensable in pond building and, fortunately, reasonably priced in rough loads. The fine-grained mineral building material makes a good pad for the pond foil. Sand is also suitable for covering the foil and mixing with substrata for water plants.

Boulders can be obtained at reasonable prices from quarries in mountainous areas. Addresses can be found in the telephone directory. Sometimes large gravel, very suitable for pond formation, turns up in the excavation of gravel pits. Sources of natural stone also include the fields in the vicinity. On request, many farmers give interested people stones that they turn up when plowing. Stones found in open areas naturally cannot simply be removed, which for large boulders can only be done with machinery anyway. In gardens that are made on stony ground, the raw materials are often there right outside the door. It pays to watch for useful stones, which might be moved aside during the building work, when a site is excavated for building a house. As long as the heavy construction machines are still on the site, transporting large boulders to another place is no problem.

Natural stone cut into cubes is used in great quantities in paving. This nice material is also of value in building water gardens, for example, in making pond edges or attaching benches by the pond. Besides gray or reddish granite, light limestone can also be had.

* Stone Instead of Wood

Frost-secure natural stone is the best building material for securing slopes. It looks natural and gives the garden or retaining wall an Alpine character. Above all, though, it is fully weather-resistant and does not rot—unlike wooden palisades, which also look very nice but, despite highly poisonous impregnation material, last only a limited time.

Costs

BASIC COSTS

The cost of a typical foil pond is modest:

Pond Foil   Pond foil (1-mm PE foil) can be bought for ca. 5 Euro per square meter.

Sand/Gravel   1 cubic meter of sand costs about 15 Euro, 1 cubic meter of gravel a little less.

Delivery   It always pays to order a larger shipment so the delivery costs (ca. 50 Euro depending on distance) are worth it. Prices on inquiry.

Suppliers   Find names of suppliers in the yellow pages. Delivery is usually right after ordering, often on the same day.

CONSTRUCTION

While a "raw pond" can be had at low cost, finishing it can be expensive.

Water Plants   Prices of water plants are between 3 and 10 Euro apiece, depending on type and size. One who has a good source or green thumb is lucky. One can often get water plants from neighbors or known pool owners, as long as they have more plants than they know what to do with. Most water plants are very hardy and need to be reduced frequently. The leftovers end up in the compost if nobody wants them. Increasing through division, shoots or seeds is not a problem either.

Machinery   Pumps, filters, and other machinery are not needed to keep a pond healthy. Of course a fountain does not work without a pump. Pump costs have their limits. A good pond pump sells for about 100 Euro. In making a choice, the operating costs need to be considered. A 100-watt pump in regular use consumes 2.4 kilowatts of power per day. That adds up in the course of a garden season! Solar pumps and the needed accessories are a lot more expensive that comparable electric pumps but have no operating costs.

Water in Action

Fountains Springs and Cascades

The babbling of a brook, the splashing of a fountain or the bubbling of a spring has a pleasant, restful effect as long as the sound is kept in moderation. In the garden, pumps and regulating systems make the strength of the flow or spray possible. Simple water action needs little mechanism otherwise. They can be set up by simple means in a courtyard, on a terrace or a balcony.

WATER RUNS DOWN SLOPES
Water Steps

Water Play for Children

Playing with water obviously gives children pleasure. So this can happen without danger, only shallow bodies of water should be placed in family gardens. Playing on home-built water steps is not a problem.

A pond needs a secure sealing or will lose its water and be turned into a sandbox. Yet the children do not need to do without the wet element. Water action that can be built by simple means is not dangerous.

For water steps, one needs a few round logs from a forest or from taking down trees of your own. Milled palisades from the garden shop are just as suitable. The round pieces are cut in half and hollowed out. This can be done with a special rounded axe that can be bought in tool shops specializing in forestry. But a chisel can also be used to form shallow waterways. The hollowed-out half-round pieces of wood each get two holes for attaching stilts. Dowels cut to fit and are attached with bolts to the half-round wood will do the job. The individual elements of the water steps must be seated firmly in the ground. On a grown-up lime soil it is enough if the steel rods are driven in some 50 cm deep. In loose humus or sandy ground, small piers of concrete are needed under some conditions. When one divides the individual stairs of the water steps, one should make sure that they are positioned correctly, so that the water splashes from step to step. So that it does not overflow, the half-round pieces of wood always have a wall on the rear end. Sealing the boreholes in which the dowels are fitted can be done with silicone. During the construction, the water flow should be checked now and then. If necessary, changes are still possible now. The water comes from a cistern via a hand pump. Rainwater costs nothing and can be used at will. The quality can be checked at times with a test set from a garden shop. An old wooden barrel serves as a rain barrel. Such containers are available as planters. From there the water runs underground to the steps. To bridge the piece of lawn between the cistern and the water steps, plastic pipes are buried in the ground. After the water is pumped into the barrel, it flows through the plastic pipes over the water steps into a gravel basin.

*The Water Finds its Way

According to the law of gravity, the water follows the quickest path from the source to the mouth. But if the steps have too little slope, it will not run off in the desired direction. This can be cured by a more sloping position of the steps, as well as by small boards that serve as closings on the back. The further extension of the steps is built step by step. Only when a test shows that the water runs right is the next step built. Make sure too that the steel pins are anchored firmly in the ground.

Using Your Own Water
Rainwater in an underground cistern is available in sufficient quantities. The concrete cistern is sunk in the ground when the house is built. The hand pump moves the water upward into the barrel by muscle power. The quality of rainwater has meanwhile become very good again. In any case, it is suitable for use in the water steps. After running into the basin at the mouth, it can be pumped back into the cistern if a pump and hose line are installed.

Left: The water steps are supplied from a wooden barrel. For this it is necessary at first to pump gathered rainwater from a cistern up into a barrel. This is done with a hand pump attached to a suction hose. To connect it, a hole must be cut into the cistern with a drill.

Lower left: The water runs out of the barrel through a plastic pipe to the wooden steps. The plastic pipe can be place3d out of sight in the ground. For it, a flat ditch is dug. After putting in the pipe, the dug-out sods are put back in place.

* **At a Glance**
Simple, but time-consuming
Tools: round axe, angle cutter, drill, hammer
One work day
Cost of the rods and bolts ca. 50 Euro.

Below: The metal pipe must reach down to the bottom of the cistern. At the bottom it is fitted with a filter, through which the water flows into the pipe. The connections must be watertight, so the pump does not suck in air. Installation is made through the opening in the concrete cistern.

Upper left: The hand pump has a base of cast iron. It must be mounted firmly. For this, a small concrete base, covered with natural stone, is needed. Instead of a complicated design, a small concrete socket suffices to fasten the pump.

Upper right: For the later connection of an electric pump to the suction tube, a distributor is mounted here. If necessary, the plug can be unscrewed, so that along with the hand pump for the water steps, an electric pump for watering the garden can be connected. At right in the picture is the plastic pipe that leads through a hole in the base into the barrel.

Lower left: The water steps are made out of prepared half-round wood, hollowed out and mounted on steel pins in the ground. During the building, it should be tested to make sure the water runs right. If necessary, the position or the slope needs to be adjusted.

Lower right: After finishing the steps and making the final water-flow test, the surroundings can be built up. Pieces of limestone can be placed on the slope. Climbing plants placed on both sides later conceal the steel pins of the structure.

DECORATIVE WATER CONTAINERS
Wells

Granite Wells

Water basins of natural stone are very well suited to be water sources in a vegetable garden, rainwater collectors or well basins in a garden.

Such hand-hewn decorative stones made of granite or other hard natural stone have their price, of course. Considerably less costly is a similar container made of granite slabs, or the building up of paving stones into an angular or round tub. Granite bars are industrial products, usually available in great quantities as curbstones in road building. They can be combined with concrete to make massive containers. More complex to build but no less massive are water basins of granite stone.

Walls with Granite Bars

The curbstones that are known to the building trade as granite slabs in Germany come in varying sizes (such as 100 x 20 x 10 cm). The cut stones generally come from China or Eastern Europe, as the costs of quarrying and shaping them are lower there than western Europe or America. Orders are delivered by truck, on wooden pallets. Transporting one of these heavy loads is also possible with a car and trailer. For a small well—as in the picture—ten pieces are sufficient. A small quantity of concrete, composed, for example, of sieved gravel, cement and water mixed in a mixer, is also needed to put them together. Ready-mixed concrete is just as suitable. The mixing of these goods can be done in a tub with an electric drill.

A suitable location for the well must be found first. It can be a place beside a rain spout that can be tapped during construction. For the flow of rainwater and the removal of water for watering, and to empty the well in the autumn, holes in the walls are needed. Working the hard granite is best done by a mason, who can cut the needed holes in marked places on the granite slabs. Such specialists use diamond-tipped drills. The cost of the exact and smooth drill holes is worth it, as one's own holes, perhaps made with a hammer, can be made only with difficulty and not without the danger of breakage. But whoever wants to bore the holes himself should first practice on a junk piece or ordinary top stone.

Making the Masonry—Step by Step

It is recommended that one set up the well first without concrete—using a drawing. To do this, set up the granite slabs at the location in the desired basin shape. Be careful when working with the heavy raw slabs. A helper should secure the already standing stones. As soon as the basis is set up, belts and boards prevent the stones from tipping. Now an evaluation can be made calmly. If one wishes, the shape and size can still be changed. In that case, more granite slabs have to be obtained. When the basin satisfies one's wishes, construction can begin. The basin is taken apart into its individual pieces and then built up with concrete. The base is formed by a concrete slab poured from fresh concrete. So the basin remains mobile and does not get attached to the pavement or other base, a dividing layer between the concrete slab and the base is necessary. A piece of foil (such as firm pond foil) spread out before the basin is

built does the job. The granite slabs can be built up on top of it. At first a thin stripe of fresh concrete is spread on the foil. Then the first granite slab is put in place. The second stone also gets a stripe of fresh concrete going sideways from where the stones meet. This can be spread well with a trowel and pressed, so that it remains joined when the granite slab is set up. Now the prepared second granite slab is attached to the already standing first one. When it is set up, the concrete is attached firmly to both slabs in the joint. The other stones are handled and erected in the same way. In this way the basin comes into being. Before setting up and attaching the last stone, pour concrete to form the bottom. In a large basin, in which the bottom can be reached later with no trouble, this can be done from above at the end. A piece of grid or steel mesh helps to strengthen the concrete bottom. It is cut to size and pressed into the fresh concrete. Now only the securing of the finished basin remains, so that the concrete can set in peace.

CASCADES
Waterfalls on Slopes or Hills

A Pond With Cascades

A dull rosebush can be livened up by a big foil pond. The excavated soil serves as a hill for a small waterfall.

A lawn beside a house is an ideal spot for children to play. Later, when it is no longer used, it can be turned into a pond. Besides, a nicely formed pond needs no more care than a lawn. The bigger the water surface is, the better effect it has. The size naturally is derived from the size of the yard. After measuring and staking the surface, the excavation begins. A small excavator saves laborious digging. The dug-out soil remains on the scene and can be piled up to form a wall around the pond. Here a small water course can splash later. After shaping the pond bed and padding it with sand and fleece (or old carpets), the pond foil can be laid out. Non-toxic PE foil can be had in all sizes. Foil one mm thick will withstand stress and weather. In flooding the pond, the building up with gravel begins. It is best to be sparing with soil and plants; otherwise the water surface is soon crowded. Some selected water plants that are set in baskets or pits are sufficient. On the other hand, the shore can be planted very richly with greenery. Boulders are needed for the watercourse. So the water splashes nicely over them and does not run under them, they must be placed carefully and layered. When everything works right and the pond is filled, the projecting edges of foil can be trimmed off. Then the water garden can grow in peace.

A sloping area or a steep slope is very suitable for a watercourse. When selected natural stones are arranged nicely, the water cascades cheerily down them. A strong flow of water does not freeze in winter.

In a garden without a natural slope, an artificial brook can be laid out on the excavated soil in the course of pond building. A wall is built up at the edge and shaped so that a favorable foundation for a watercourse is formed. Here the rough work is already done by a small excavator. After shaping the pond bed and building up a hill of earth on the shore, the job is well underway already.

While gravel is used in building a pond, and large pieces of stone are used only here and there in formation, the building of a brook is done with selected stones. The water must run when the first stone is set. This shows whether it is runs visibly and audibly over the stones or runs ineffectively between them. The steeper the slope, the more easily the stones can be arranged favorably.

The water can collect in small puddles and then run down to the next basin over small steep places. Before covering with pond foil, these basins and steps should be shaped. If necessary, soil can be filled in later in places. But that must be done before putting in gravel and large stones. The book and cascades already begin to take on their clear form.

In a small area, a really effective watercourse can be built in this way with little use of materials, and can look particularly natural. Selected shrubs add to the formation. Angled slabs of stone, such as water building stones of granite or slate, can be piled up more simply than round stones to form cascades. But the construction must be done step by step, so that the water flows along over them and does not vanish into the cracks. If necessary, hollows can be filled in with concrete and covered with gravel.

Soon after installation, the water clears. The formerly monotone water surface has turned into an attractive water garden. Naturally, such bodies of water can also be combined with lawns as long as there is enough room for both in a small garden. For greenery, of course, only shrubs and small tress that do not grow too big are suitable. The water surface should remain free, so that it still has its effect years later.

SMALL BODIES OF WATER

Birdbaths in the Garden

Helping Animals Survive

On hot summer days, birds fly to garden fruits to quench their thirst. Without water, cherries and berries refresh them. A water source can help keep birds away from the fruit but keep the animals in the garden.

Flat basin-shaped stones, ceramic or clay basins are formative elements that can be used in many places. Not only do flowers, shrubs or even trees grow in the spaces; the natural—or sometimes hand-carved—boulders are very useful for birdbaths.

> * **Effective Locating**
> Birdbaths, like birdhouses, can be placed high on pedestals to decrease danger from prowling cats.

On hot summer days, our feathered friends fly in from all sides to quench their thirst. Some even come to bathe. Blackbirds and sparrows land unabashed in the basins, spread out their wings and dip into the cool liquid. In sheltered places with free flyways and open fields of vision, even shy birds show up.

Birdbaths serve not only feathered guests, but also serve as decorations. Hand-hewn natural stones or basins made of clay can be added to a garden scene very tastefully. Make sure that ceramic basins are not always impervious to frost. They must be baked at high temperatures. A glaze prevents water loss. Easily breakable material can be used elsewhere if larger pets, particularly dogs, jump into the basin.

Care

Natural stones last in open air, where wind, rain, light and finally, over the years, green moss affect the surface. Basins need regular care. On hot days, evaporated water needs to be replaced during regular watering, falling leaves and algae need to be removed. If need be, unfavorably set-up basins can be set right.

WATER COLLECTING PLACES
Springs, Fountains, and Water Suppliers

Locating Water Basins in the Garden

Even small bodies of water have a value in the garden as decorative basins, birdbaths or sources of water. They can be small springs that are very audible and visible on a terrace, or bubbling fountains that, perhaps with the help of solar energy, produce a strong flow of water, or just simple water containers in which fresh water is always ready for songbirds to drink and bathe, or sources of water for watering the garden.

The size, shape and type of such bodies of water depend on their uses. Even a simple mortar tub can have a value as a decorative body of water if it is sunk out of sight in the ground beside an herb garden and hidden with natural stones. Wooden barrels set up as springs by means of small pumps do not need to be hidden. Old wine and liquor barrels cam be had for reasonable prices in building and garden shops. The boards swell up after being filled with water, so that the barrels become watertight again. If necessary, a covering of thin pond foil

can provide secure leak-proofing if the barrels have large holes. Whoever has an old sheet-zinc bathtub in the cellar or finds one at the dump can also use it as a spring or a mini-pond. This is also true of feeding troughs of clay or natural stone that can sometimes be found in natural stone dealers or garden shops. Water basins can also be cast in concrete, with the use of a form, for use as water supply sources, springs or birdbaths. The form can be made of boards or by using plastic tubs.

Water does not need large ponds; it can have a good effect even in small containers. Selected watertight vessels, particularly of natural materials, are well suited for this. Even plants do well in such water containers. The water is refreshing with it is brought into motion by a pump. A suitable place for a bubbling fountain can be found beside a two-seat bench or a pond.

Biotopes

Bodies of Water are Living Places

Biotopes are living spaces for specialized plants and animals. Different types settle on dry lawns than on constantly wet or sometimes flooded places. The "water garden" biotope is an ideal place for native trees and shrubs that also thrive in nature on the shores of rivers, brooks of lakes. If the living space suits them, the typical animals also come to it. A multi-faceted biotope with bodies of water, landing zones, gravel surfaces and rock gardens offers favorable living conditions for a variety of plants and animals.

WET BIOTOPES FOR ANIMALS AND PLANTS
Many Like Wetness

Water for All

Water is just as important for animals as for people. One or, better, several bodies of water considerably encourage the settling of birds, insects and other users.

Breeding birds need only return from short flights to supply their young with food. That makes the laborious job of raising a brood easier for them. When a natural body of water is in the vicinity, they can always have a full supply. If not, artificial waters like garden ponds, fountains or birdbaths help them. A pond also offers them further advantages. Here the animals find not only the necessary drinking water, but among other things, also building material to line their nests with grass and luxuriant water plants. In addition, the body of water invites them to bathe. Besides the song birds, many crawling animals and insects whose lives are made easier, other animals are fully dependent on water. They include frogs, salamanders, fish, and, naturally, insects like dragonflies, water striders and water bugs. For such animals, a wet biotope (from the

Greek *bios*, life) is necessary for life. This is also true of plants that are specialized for wet locations, such as water lilies and mare's tails, which constantly live underwater, or for reeds, rushes and swamp iris, which sometimes need a flooding.

Vital water plants need large long-term bodies of water that can handle their urge to spread out. Swamp iris grow luxuriantly in shallow water, while rushes push forward into the ponds from shallow water.

THE SWAMP, A SPECIAL BIOTOPE
Nutrient-Rich Water Gardens

A Swamp in the Garden?

The swamp flora are characterized by a particular vitality. This should be kept in mind when laying out a garden pond, as the small water surface will otherwise be fully overgrown. Reeds, rushes and other invasive swamp plants are held back in containers or by barriers. It may be that they would thrive luxuriantly and deliberately take over a body of water. Your own swamp basin with attractive swamp plants may be recommended as an addition to a pond, if it is to remain open—without thick shore vegetation. The swamp basin is then supplied with water by the pond when excess rainwater overflows into it. This is usually enough, as long as the swamp plants can stand water variation and occasional dryness.

Laying Out the Surface

The bigger a swamp basin is made, the more stable and, naturally, more valuable it is, because many kinds of plants can spread out. Swamp plants naturally grow in small containers as well, but they have the best effect in groups on flat areas.

Swamp Plants (selection)

Sweet flag (*Acorus calamus*), water plantain (*Alisma plantago-aquatica*), flowering rush (*Butomus umbellatus*), water arum (*Calla palustris*), marsh marigold (*Caltha palustris*), sedge (*Carex sp.*) umbrella sedge (*Cyperus longus*), cotton grass (*Eriophorum*), mare's tail (*Hippuris vulgaris*), water violet (*Hottonia palustris*), swamp iris (*Iris sp.*), rush (*Juncus*), loosestrife (*Lysimachia sp.*), purple loosestrife (*Lythrum salicaria*), water mint (*Mentha aquatica*), bog bean (*Menyanthes trifoliate*), forget-me-not (*Myosotis palustris*), watercress (*Nasturtium officinale*), reed (*Phragmites australis*) buttercup (*Ranunculus lingua*), arrowhead (*Sagittaria*), clubrush (*Scirpus lacustris*), bulrush (*Typha sp.*), brooklime (*Veronica beccabunga*).

Wet Zones for Greedy Plants

Swamp zones belong to rivers and lakes as water does. Swamps arise through deposits of the finest minerals and organic materials in quiet shore zones, on the bottom or in bays. Swamp zones house their own flora and fauna, which need the damp environment to live.

The rivers and brooks move clear water mainly in their upper reaches, where the swift current allows no deposits. Similarly, in lakes it is usually only the water at the top that is clear. Otherwise these bodies of water are more or less murky. Where the sediments are deposited and thick layers of mud are formed, swamp zones arise.

Construction

A swamp can be laid out very well on a lime or clay soil if the soil is stamped or thickened with a vibrator. But a lime or clay bed is not completely watertight and needs regular watering in dry spells. Just as in building a pond, pond foil is useful here. It is best bought in one piece to avoid gluing. To protect the foil, a padding of pond fleece or sand is recommended. Working with the soil—as in building a pond—is best done by hand for a small basin. A mini-excavator helps with a large basin. But the swamp bed remains shallower than a pond and requires less effort. A deep spot of some 60 to 80 cm is advisable, so that overwintering animals can withdraw in case of a hard frost. Otherwise 20 to 40 cm of depth will suffice, as long as the native swamp plants can stand frost. Part of the excavated soil is sometimes set aside and then filled in again after the foil is laid. Unlike a pond, it may supply nourishment. The swamp plants then thrive all the better. A few plants are sufficient for a large basin. Above all, strongly growing types like rushes or reeds should be planted very sparingly, so they will be less of a threat to the less dominant marsh marigolds, swamp iris or mare's tail. The still visible foil is covered with soil and/or gravel. This conceals and protects it. After covering, filling and planting, it can be flooded, at first with tap or spring water. Later the overflow from the pond is usually enough, if the latter is supplied with rainwater from the roof. Finally, it is necessary to cut off the foil edges and plant the banks with grass and shrubs. A swamp does not need special care. It is enough to water it in dry weather and remove dead plant parts. Sometimes invasive plants can also be cut back. Just as the swamp zones in a pond do not smell very bad, the swamp does not spread bad smells. Foul gases result only when there is digging in the mud.

Swimming Pools, Wading Pools, and Kneipp Basins

Refreshing Bodies of Water

Whoever lives on a lake or a river can plunge into the water at any time in the summer. But one's own garden also invites bathing if a body of water is created. This can be a pool or a swimming pond. For refreshing, for Kneipp bathing or as a wading pool for the children, even a plastic pool placed on the lawn on hot summer days suffices.

ENJOYABLE BODIES OF WATER

Ponds to Take a Dip in

Open-air Pools in Your Own Garden

A real swimming pool naturally needs a certain surface area and enough depth for sufficient freedom of movement. So a practical construction is necessary. In particular, the pond basin must be safe from damage or protected.

Building a swimming pool is in itself possible with typical pond foil. After being covered, it receives a protective coat of gravel. Pond foil can be ordered in any size in the trade. Avoid making your own seams in it. The pond bed must be excavated deeply and spaciously enough. This is done most simply with a mini-excavator. It is then built up like a foil pond. First a layer of building sand is put into the pit. Then the foil is spread on top of it. It disappears under a layer of gravel (usually small). Plants should be set in sparingly; otherwise the pond will become overgrown in time. It is best to plant robust types like reeds, swamp iris and rushes. Such a foil pond is relatively inexpensive to build. It offers enough play room for swimming if it is made big enough. A pump with a filter attached provides water. Rainwater can also serve to supply it if a drainpipe from the roof is tapped into. For this, there are simple water collectors with suction connectors available in building stores. A small bathing pool can also be made out of hard plastic parts. The commercially available pond basins naturally offer much less freedom of motion than larger foil ponds, since their size is limited. But such bodies of water are very suitable as wading pools for children, or for Kneipp basins. Concrete components, otherwise used to build wells and cisterns, have also proved themselves. Concrete rings can be had in diameters up to about 300 cm. They can be set in the ground by a crane truck. Naturally, a suitable pit of the desired depth has to be dug out first. Waterproofing materials can be painted on the inside walls to seal them. Before building a real swimming pool, estimates of the cost should be obtained. A small professionally built swimming pool can cost more than 10,000 Euro!

The plastic basin with gravel serves as a wading pool; later the gravel is removed and it can be changed into a water garden.

The "Water Test" is fun on hot summer days during the building and flooding. The cold water from a well, or from the pipes, naturally needs some time before it clears and all the sediments stirred up from the gravel settle to the bottom. The sand and gravel, though, do not decrease the quality. Later too, the swimming pool regularly receives fresh water from its own source or from the water pipes.

BUILDING A SWIMMING POOL

A Body of Water by the House

Pond Building in the Course of Garden Formation

The building of a swimming pool with a rich plant biotope should already be considered when planning the house and garden. Then there are still ways for heavy vehicles like excavators and trucks to get in.

Hard and laborious excavating work by hand or with a mini-excavator can thus be avoided. Particularly in rough terrain, such as with rocks underground or clay soil, the use of an excavator is worthwhile, finishing the excavation for a deep pond in a short time with its big jaws. The dug-out soil, or—depending on the yard situation—another usable material like sand, gravel or natural stone, can be used in the job of forming the garden and for walls around the pond, or for building a dry wall. Too much, or unsuitable dug-out material, pieces of stone or heavy lime soil can be taken away in the builders' truck. Depending on its composition, it can be used for road building, filling in gravel pits, or other projects.

In the pictures, the excavator digs up broken limestone that proved to be not impervious to frost and thus could only be partially used in the garden. Among other things, it was used to build a privacy wall on the property line, now the home of a wild hedge. The slightly inclined location made a large-scale excavation for the garden area necessary. The pond should never be a

Far left: The loose stones that the excavator unearths will be taken away by truck.

Left: Where the water will flow in the pond, the work begins with cement from a mixer.

Lower left: The foundation can be poured in the ground without a form; it provides a massive base for the subsequent structure.

Lower center: After the concrete base hardens, building the frame can be done. The pieces are being placed.

Below: The assembly proceeds quickly with special clamps. The necessary pieces have to be chosen correctly by the borrower.

security risk for the house—not even in extreme situations, such as after heavy rain. Here the decision was made for a concrete support wall that in any case will stand up to the pressure of the water over time. The steep angular walls that thus came into being made an unusual terrace formation possible. The space between the house and the concrete wall forms a large bridge that can be used as a sitting place right by the pond. The pond by the house has the effect of a valuable formative element all year, being reachable in a few steps and easy to see from the living rooms even in winter. To shield it from view from the house next door and also from the wind, a massive wall of larch wood was built. It also serves as a climbing place for a wisteria and a trumpet vine. The post anchors for the shielding wall could be set in fresh concrete during the course of construction. Through the concrete walls, a small inner courtyard was also created next to the pond and secured with a support wall of concrete.

The building of concrete support walls requires a stable form that can withstand the pressure of the fresh concrete. Such systems can be rented from building firms or other renters. The heavy wooden parts and the attachments require a lot of pressure. The building site must be prepared well before the form is erected. In one case, after the pit was excavated, massive sockets of concrete were cast, forming a solid base for the forms after they hardened. Before the forms are ordered, a drawing that shows the lengths and heights is needed. According to it, suitable pieces can be obtained from the form renter. In the same way, the quantities of concrete and structural steel can be calculated. For large support walls, the use of ready-mixed concrete, transported directly to the building site and pumped into the form by a concrete pump, is worthwhile. Smaller quantities can be prepared in a cement mixer.

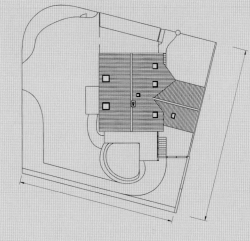

A plan of the house with exact dimensions is also useful for garden forma-tion. The first designs are made on copies of the plan. Planning on a computer is also possible after the layout and other details have been transferred to it. Here the position, shape and size of the pond are already deter-mined.

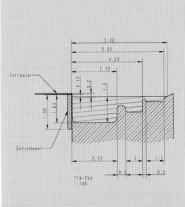

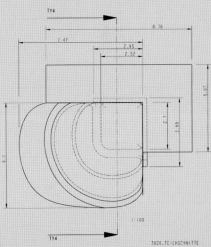

The support walls, built with the help of forms, are in principle just comparatively thin concrete lines or angles. The advantage of the con-crete construction is that extremely stable elements can be built with little material, and can be laid out as desired.

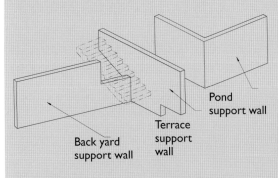

Back yard support wall

Terrace support wall

Pond support wall

Volumes: 2.2 cu.m. + 2.2 cu.m. + 3 cu.m. = 7.4 cubic meters

The pond is divided into three zones. The deep-water area for swimming begins right by the terrace; behind a wall is the area for water lilies, and the shallow-water zone is right after that. The proportions are matched to the terrace area and garden size.

Above: It is possible to prepare concrete with the help of a mixer on the site; gravel, cement and water are needed.

Upper left: The steel grids give the concrete walls the firmness they need. They must be installed precisely.

Lower left: Setting up the structural steel is done step-by-step with the erection of the forms. Then the grids are cut to fit.

Below: So-called gap holders—special plastic pipes—hold the forms at the right distance; steel rods give the needed stability.

* **Oiling the Forms**
The forms for concrete walls can be removed more easily after the concrete hardens if the parts are coated with oil before the concrete is poured. This special oil is available from a building supply store or the renter of the forms.

The gravel and cement for the job are obtained before the concrete is mixed. The structural steel for the support walls can be had from a building material dealer. Steel grids and rods are needed for reinforcement. They must be put in carefully. So that the steel elements are located firmly inside the cast concrete and do not stick out later, gap holders are needed to separate them from the forms. Whoever has little experience with such massive concrete elements should always get advice from a specialist. If the concrete walls were not included in the plans for building the house, an acceptable plan must usually be submitted to the local building office. A preliminary inquiry is advisable if the pond project goes to unusual dimensions or if complaints from neighbors may be anticipated. The conditions are published in the building requirements of the state. For example, according to the Bavarian regulations, walls with a height up to 1.80 meters inside the property do not need approval. Permission is not needed for swimming pools up to 100 cubic meters. The building office will give information.

As soon as the forms are put together from separate pieces and the steel reinforcement is put in, pouring the concrete can begin. Air bubbles in the concrete can be avoided by shaking with a vibrator. The motor-driven steel rod creates oscillations and spreads the concrete evenly between the form walls. For less massive walls, stamping by hand can also be of help. As soon as the forms are filled, the concrete just needs to be smoothed with a trowel. If necessary, ground covers, such as for a privacy wall or post anchors for a pergola must be inserted in the still-soft concrete. That avoids later attachment by boring holes. The metal elements are held in the hardening concrete and are then firmly mounted in the wall. Or bottles can be inserted into the concrete. They are then removed at the right time, as soon as the concrete has hardened. The resulting pods can then hold post anchors, fence posts or other attachments. As soon as the concrete

has hardened for a few days, the forms can be removed.

Bits of concrete are removed from the pieces of the forms before they are ready to be returned. The renter either picks them up, or they are left ready to be loaded onto a truck trailer. In the course of their removal, the concrete wall becomes visible. The steel reinforcements are hidden inside the concrete, providing the necessary firmness.

Building the base of the pond continues after preparing the support walls with the building of two low interior walls to separate the plant biotope from the swimming pool. Low walls built of concrete blocks are sufficient. These walls, like the big support walls, are reinforced with steel. Steel rods put in vertically do the job after the bottoms of the concrete blocks are penetrated with a hammer. In the building material trade, special concrete blocks with small closed bottoms can be had. They can be filled with concrete like an ordinary block after construction and held with vertical steel rods. There are also troughs that allow the horizontal laying of structural steel rods.

Making Connections

As soon as the angled walls are standing, the two sides have to be lengthened, as show in the photos. This is done with homemade forms made of boards and covers. Along with the big support wall, the small inside wall forms the basis for the further building of the swimming pool. Next comes the setting up of the needed connections. For water supply from the cellar and from a rainwater cistern by the house, a PE duct is laid. Excess water is removed through a plastic tube that is assembled from available parts.

Top: The individual parts of the forms make a quick assembly possible; the forms must be completely tight. Cover plates or old boards can be out into place and held by screw clamps.

Upper left: Only when the form is up and well secured can it be filled with fresh concrete. The steel grids are secured by special plastic parts.

Above: When the concrete is poured, the post anchors for the privacy wall can be inserted into the fresh concrete. Pieces of wood hold them in the right positions.

Left: It takes several days before the concrete is hardened. Then the forms can be removed. Vibrating while pouring the concrete makes the walls smooth.

Second from bottom: The inside walls for the swimming pool are made of concrete blocks. They are built up on narrow strip foundations. The concrete wall is painted with bitumen to seal it from moisture.

Bottom: The concrete walls have to be lengthened on both sides to give them their planned length. Scrap wood suffices for the forms.

Above: To supply the pool with water and electric power, and to drain it, conduits need to be laid next to the finished concrete walls. The wall is also given wall protection made of plastic.

Upper left: After the conduits are laid and the pond is filled, the substructure by the house can be vibrated. The plastic pipes themselves bear the pressure of heavy machines when they are laid in a bed of sand.

To keep the conduits reachable, which is necessary later for the attachment of water dividers and other equipment, a shaft of concrete rings is built. Such shaped pieces are available in varying sizes in the trade.

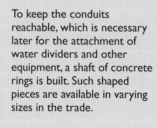

Below: It is best to have the heavy concrete rings brought to the scene by heavy machinery, though moving them by rolling is possible. After setting in place, they must be absolutely horizontal.

These so-called KG pipes are available in various lengths at building supply stores, along with corners and sealers. Do not forget ground cables to provide power at the pond and, if desired, on into the garden, such as for lighting or for a nearby shed. They are laid in a bed of sand parallel to the water pipes. A suitable meeting place is a shaft built of concrete rings in a handy position near the pond. These shaped concrete pieces, in various sizes, are also available in the trade. Beside the shaft for the connections there is a gully for overflowing water from the pond. For it, a shallow ditch was dug out when the support wall was built. The water then runs over this deep spot on the shore into the gully, such as after heavy rain, and flows through the drainpipe to the cistern. An excavator driver who is working with the soil on the site can help install it. He fills the pits neat the pond with gravel that forms the foundation for a pavement of plates. The ditch between the house and the support wall, which is filled in here, can also be used sometimes as storage space. If a wooden terrace is wanted instead of a paved area, the space between the house and support wall can be bridged by timbers. These serve to support the wooden planks. The pit under the wooden terrace must be prepared appropriately before removal. Access is possible later through a hatch in the wooden floor.

Substructure for Pavement

For a surface of paving stones or slabs, a strong substructure is necessary. Rock rubble or gravel that has been thickened with a vibration plate or tamper does the job. Depending on the terrace pavement, a layer of fine gravel is spread over it for a small-format paving, or thin concrete if large slabs are to be used.

Laying the pavement comes only later, as soon as the foil is laid on the pond bed. Only then can the angled steel profiles [?] be screwed onto the concrete support wall. They hold the foil fast and also form closing angles for the pavement.

Preparing Pond Foil

The pond foil is ordered from a manufacturer as a single piece. Exact measurements and drawings of the pond shape and diameter are needed. Measurement is done with a measuring tape. For the exact length and width of the pond bed, 50 cm more on each side should be added. The overhanging edges can be buried under the gravel layer or, where they are in the way, trimmed off after the pond has been dressed. The manufacturer produces the fitting foil in the needed size out of pieces according to the measurements and drawings. It is systematically rolled up according to a certain pattern and then sent by express. At the building site, the heavy roll is taken to the prepared pond bed by main strength or, if possible, by machinery. The marking on the foil packaging should be followed. It shows how the foil is folded and should be rolled out.

Padding the Pond Bed

So that the pond foil is not permanently exposed to any pressure, such as from pointed stones or roots, the stony pond bed needs a padding of sand. A layer some 10 cm thick forms an effective protection from pressure. The sand is also ideal for forming plateaus in the pond bed. It can be spread easily and worked into channels, slopes or flat surfaces. During the pond padding, the borders are also set. A laser water scale or hose scale helps here to make exact height measurements possible. As fixed points when measuring, concrete blocks can be of use.

Above: As soon as the infrastructure is built, the excavator goes into action. The big shovel does the filling in a few work processes. Naturally, the work can also be done by hand. But using the machine allows the excavated soil to be arranged in the pond bed or otherwise.

Upper right: Do not forget a spillway for the overflow. A shaped concrete piece, later fitted with a gully, can also be used here. The water overflow pipes lead to a cistern by the house.

Center: After installing the dividing and safety systems, the work of laying the pavement begins. Using a vibration compressor prevents the substructure from sinking later.

Right: Independent of the work outside at the pond, preparations inside the walls can proceed. The procedure depends on the time for building the pond, the delivery of the materials, and not least on the builder's schedule.

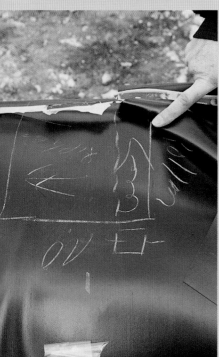

Above: If the surrounding garden area is not yet finished, concrete blocks can be used to set up the final shore height.

Upper left: To order the pond foil, the measurements must be known. Fixed points make measuring easier.

Right: Delivering the foil, slope mats and fleece generally takes place shortly after they are ordered.

Left: A simple drawing on the foil roll shows how the foil is folded. This drawing must be kept in mind when the foil is laid out.

Below: It is a good idea to measure the fleece dimensions with a little to spare, as this acrylic fiber material protects the foil from pressure, especially on stony ground.

They show the course and height of the ponds banks. Later they are replaced by sand in the course of forming the pond shore. Additional protection for the foil is provided by a layer of pond fleece, which is cut to fit after being rolled out and spread out on the sand padding. Covering with this non-decaying acrylic fiber matting is worthwhile in critical places like the wall angles, or on steep slopes where sand trickles away.

Unrolling the Foil

If the foil lies properly after being unrolled, spreading it out causes no problems. But several people should help, as the plastic foil, 1 mm thick, weighs several hundredweights. After being unrolled into the pond bed, the foil on the opposite shore must be rolled or pulled up again. On steep slopes this can only be done by several people. According to how it is folded, the foil can then be pulled out to both sides and spread out on the surface. While folds on the pond bed are scarcely noticed, as they disappear later under the gravel, a large fold is formed on an angular steep wall. This must be smoothed out as much as possible and pressed onto the wall. No tension spots or open spaces must form behind the foil. The folding must be done very carefully, especially in the corners. Cutting off part of the excess foil on the edges makes folding and smoothing much easier. Of course it must not be cut too short, as the water pressure will pull the edges downward.

Test Period

The pictures show the pond being flooded as a test. For safety reasons, the water must be removed again. Only after the property is fenced in can the planting and then the flooding be done. Only in this way can the danger of playing neighborhood

children having an accident be avoided. During the test period after the foil is installed, a keep-out line and warning sign indicate danger concerning the pond. Such optical limits should naturally afford safety.

During the test period it is shown that the full-sun position encouraged strong algae growth. The luxuriant growth of algae was [no main verb] through the lack of gravel, plants, animals and microorganisms, which contribute to filtering an established pond. The installation of a filter with a pump can solve such problems, though a properly laid-put swimming pool should function without technology. Here it should be noted that every body of water develops its own dynamics. As soon as a pond, basin or other body of water is flooded, plants and animals settle there on their own and affect the water quality. Many other factors also make themselves known, such as the situation (sunny or shady), the properties of the water (pH value, oxygen content, etc.), the vegetation (such as nearby trees, shrubs on the shore), and the season (for example, installation in spring or autumn). In the depicted example, a spring heat wave combined with unusually high pollen encouraged algae formation greatly.

Pool Shore Formation

The formation and construction of a water garden depends, among other things, on the availability of specialists. When special jobs are given to firms or specialists contribute to the job, their time planning should be kept in mind. Mason friends had time to do the paving during the planned setting up of the pond. The pond building was accordingly slowed in favor of building the terrace. The decision was made, after seeing various materials, in favor of large concrete paving stones, which were laid on thin concrete after delivery.

Above: the heavy roll of foil is dragged to the pond bed with difficulty. Here the excavator can be very helpful.

Upper right: After unrolling according to plan, spreading out is done easily by hand. Folding at steep walls, of course, causes difficulties.

Right: On hot days the foil can be laid more easily than in cool weather; the black plastic is less stiff and fits the bottom better.

Below: Water pressure pushes the foil firmly against the pre-formed pond bed; during flooding it must be noted that no tension forms, especially in the steep areas.

Above: To attach the pool foil and also as a holder for the terrace pavement, a metal angle bar was mounted. Later a wooden step will be installed on the water side.

Upper left: The pavement needs a strong substructure. Thin concrete, applied dry and leveled with the help of a metal bar, does the job.

Left: The prepared surface offers a completely level foundation for laying the large concrete plates. After being sprayed with water, they bond with the concrete. Thus the finished pavement is sprayed amply with water.

Below: Then mortar is applied to fasten the pavement. The bond can also be made—unlike here—with dry mortar. This is then swept into the gaps with a broom and moistened afterward.

"Teaching Time" at the Pond

While the pavement is being laid, the development in the pond can be observed. Although the water level dropped, this was not because of damage to the foil. It was rather the unusual heat during the building time that caused heavy evaporation of the water. The fully sunny weather also resulted in an unusually strong growth of algae. Just as unpleasant was the great number of gnat larvae that could obviously develop well in the pond without being threatened by hostile insects. The test, rich with lessons, finally ended with the emptying of the pond. The realization that a body of water develops so unhappily in an unfavorable place without the addition of gravel and plants was worth the test. In addition, the test flooding served to test the pond foil. The water was pumped back into the cistern, where it was available for watering the garden or being used to supply water to the pond after it was finished.

Setting Up the Pond

After the foil is cleaned from deposits, coconut mats are spread on the slopes and a special plastic material on the steep areas, then comes the preparation of the pond. The foil gradually disappears under a layer of gravel. Only on the walls of the swimming area does the bare foil remain in sight. Lattice grids are planned to cover it; they can be put in at any time in case the foil does not look good after flooding.

Using Shaped Parts

Shaped concrete parts that can be had in many shapes and sizes from a building materials store can be used to set up plant basins for invasive species or as steps or seats in and beside the pond. A ladder was not used, since access to the swimming pool is possible via concrete rings. The rings, set in a step-like order, were filled with concrete and decorated with small gravel. The same concrete rings were planted with water lilies. For this, they were placed 60 cm deep in the plant area of the pond. To protect the pond foil, the rings were given a base of small leftover pieces of foil.

Further Shore Development

While excavating the pond bed, the digger brought up not only lime soil with broken pieces of limestone, but also larger limestone boulders. These lovely natural rocks with many flint inclusions were set aside for the time. After the pond was built, they were intended to be used for building a dry wall on the slope. The available rocks were added to by excavated material from a nearby building site. In this was a massive wall came into being at no cost. Only the excavator time had to be paid for. The excavator was also useful for the soil work, evening the lawn area, and removing unwanted leftovers.

A Gravel Bed by the Pond

Most home gardens do not offer much room for a pond. In the pictures too, the space chosen between the terrace and the south edge of the property is not very large. Between the dry wall, which braces the slope right on the boundary, and the pond there still had to be a passage to the vegetable garden or inside yard. For this, a gravel bed, bordering on the pond was planned.

Above: Above: Independently of the pavement building, the pond construction proceeds. To protect and hide the foil, gravel is used. This material can be had in several sizes. Smaller sizes are more pleasant to step on (such as in a Kneipp basin).

Center: A wooden or stainless steel stairway was not used. The deep-water zone can be reached just as well on several steps made of concrete rings. They are installed on a thin bed of concrete.

Right: After setting them and filling them with concrete, the steps can be topped with small, "foot-friendly" gravel. The surface is later visible in the water.

Meanwhile the gravel bed by the pond has already taken on a clear shape. For this, a smaller grade of gravel than that in the pond has been delivered. The choice of the gravel grade depends on its use. Sand can also be used, such as when a dune is to be built instead of a gravel bed, or when children (who can swim!) want a play area by the water.

While the excavator is busy with moving soil and building the dry walls, the forming of the pond banks goes on. The shrub beds are given rims of granite stone. The gravel in the pond must still be spread.

The flat area of colorful gravel adds considerably to the formation of the pond area and makes it look larger. Pond fleece or special weed mats, which were spread out on the ground before spreading the gravel, hold invasive weeds back and make care easier. The readily visible formation benefits songbirds. They have no trouble reaching the water and can quench their thirst or take a bath without danger from prowling cats.

Enclosing Beds

The few plant areas by the pond in which selected trees, shrub,s and grasses grow receive strict borders made of granite stone. These bed borders are set on concrete and linked by concrete. After filling with sieved garden humus, they are then planted with various decorative shrubs, flowers or grasses. The lawn is similarly bordered from the pond. After spreading and grading, the curved line of granite stones is solidly in the ground and forms an effective barrier for spreading grasses. The enclosure for the bordering vegetable garden on the east side was made higher. It also serves as a support wall for the humus soil, which was filled in about knee-high.

Lawns by the Pond

Soil Work

Whoever has natural humus soil lying around should protect it during the work on the house, and move it aside, and store it if necessary. If bad soil, like heavy clay soil or, as in the picture, stony lime soil forms the natural topsoil in the garden, a thorough soil improvement or exchange of soil is recommended. For both the vegetable garden and the lawn, sieved humus was obtained and, after excavation and transportation of the soil, spread evenly on the ground by the excavator. An experienced excavator operator can do this work in a short time with a humus shovel. Spreading it with the excavator can also be done without compacting the soil. A wheel loader or mini-loader, on the other hand, leaves deep tire ruts in the ground when it pushes and spreads the soil. After such machines are used, the garden area must be loosened deeply with a heavy milling tool.

Fine Leveling

You can do the fine leveling yourself after the soil is spread. A good rake is needed for this. It can be a wooden or metal rake, or one with plastic tines, but it must have a straight bar. This makes even raking of the area possible. You also need a wheelbarrow and a shovel to gather and remove rocks, sods, and other junk, or bury them in the ground. This tool, like others, is part of the garden equipment for daily use and is usually already on hand.

Grass Seed

After leveling comes seeding. It is done most simply by machine. A motorized seeder accomplishes the ground contact, sowing the seeds, covering them with soil, and the final rolling in one work process.

Above: An experienced excavator operator prepares the lawn area in a short time, without compacting the soil. With the humus shovel, the delivered substratum is smoothed in the process of spreading.

Center: The fine smoothing is best done with a rake. If present, disturbing stones, weed roots, and the like are removed from the surface.

Left: Sowing, covering, and rolling can be done by a lawn-seeding machine in one work process. Then the ground is raked to encourage germination and even growth.

With good care, the lawn will grow evenly in a few days. A fine fluff is visible already after about ten days. It usually takes several weeks to form a carpet. Regular mowing encourages the formation of strong grass tufts.

Seeding the lawn can be done either by hand or with a fertilizer spreader. To dig the seed into the ground, a spiked roller is handy. The steel spikes press some of the seeds into the ground and roll the others lightly in. Thus the seeds reach different depths, and that is favorable for germination. Pressing the seeds is done by a roller that can be rented. The usual steel garden rollers can be filled with water to make them much heavier. They press the soil with the seeds in it and form optimal ground cover (contact of seeds with soil). In small areas, a flat shovel is sufficient. After pressing in the seeds, watering is important. Various sprinklers can be had. They promote germination, encourage thick growth, and are also useful later.

Mowing

About ten days after seeding (depending on the weather), the first green fringe of grass is visible. In the days that follow, the fresh surface needs care and enough water. Only when strong green blades of grass have developed is it time for the first mowing. The lawnmower should have a well-sharpened blade, so that it cuts the grass evenly. When a new mower is bought, its performance and operation should be suited to the lawn, and naturally also to the "operating personnel". As with every garden device, the price-performance relationship of a lawnmower should also be noted. It is a long-term purchase, and it pays to buy a good brand. Test results from a professional testing institute are useful in determining which mower to purchase. Often good mowers are offered at reasonable prices, so comparisons should always be made.

Watering During the Season

Normally, every lawn makes do with natural precipitation, as long as it rains enough in the main sprig and early summer growing seasons and the ground is still saturated from the winter. In summer, the lawn can take hot spells. Brown spots may appear, but they become green again after the next rain. Watering is unnecessary, and an extravagance—at least with drinking water. But if you want to have an ever-green carpet, collecting rainwater in a big cistern or tapping ground water with a well is practical. This should be decided on when the house is built, when the groundwork is not yet finished, but it is possible at any time afterward.

Simple sprinklers suffice to spread the water that was collected when it rained. They receive the water through a hose from the cistern, via a pump. As soon as the sprinkled lawn is deeply saturated, turn off the sprinkler. One such sprinkler is normally sufficient. Various types can be had in the trade.

---

* The Right Watering

A sufficient water supply is especially necessary after seeding the lawn. The seeds can be left lying for days without watering (naturally, they will not germinate), but as soon as the seeds are moistened (such as after a rain shower), they must be kept moist constantly. Otherwise, the tender seedlings will dry out. The smallest lawns can be watered with a watering can, and larger ones also by hand with a garden hose or, in the case of big lawns, with a lawn sprinkler.

The sprinklers have to be suitable for the lawn surface. Two of them do the job for this rectangular plot. The water comes from the cistern and is pumped upward by a household pumping system. Using sprinklers naturally depends on the weather.

The post anchors for the privacy wall were already set in the support wall when the concrete was poured (see photo). The larch beams can then be mounted at any time during the terrace building. They give the rustic larchwood wall the needed support. A steel pipe also affords a place for wisteria to climb.

Larchwood Privacy Wall

Being watched while swimming or sunbathing is unwanted. For this reason the terrace has a large privacy wall made of larch boards. The long board wall stretches from the wall of the house far out into the garden. Thus it also helps to keep cold wind away and improve the climate in the water garden. Climbing plants that ascend a specially mounted steel pipe relax the effect of the big wooden walls with green leaves.

Awnings not just for Summer Days

A rolled-up cloth roof—that is used for a marquee—is especially valuable in changeable weather. When clouds and sun alternate, this shadow-maker can be rolled up or unrolled easily. It can even do it automatically with the help of a special mechanism.

Obviously, the military had problems with the heat. So the idea of building a marquee could have come originally from this profession. In any case, the literal translation of "marquee"—"overtent of the officer's tent"—suggests it. Hot heads cannot think clearly and will do damage, not only in battle. Hot heads also often make a peaceful garden party on a terrace difficult. Cool drinks and shady seating offer protection. Of course the sun should be darkened only sometimes. In our climatic zones, nice sunny hours are fairly rare. Only in need, when our radiant star delivers too much heat, is protection wanted. If need be, a sunshade or marquee can bring the desired relief. The providers of shade are quickly folded or rolled up again when clouds darken the sun. Then a marquee vanishes into its recess. This sun protection is least obtrusive when it is mounted on a wall without a socket. So that it also functions reliably and moves in and out properly, it requires high-priced equipment and a practical mounting. As with many utensils for daily use, getting long-lasting high quality products for a marquee pay for themselves. The expensive sun-sail must always be ready for use and able to withstand any weather all year round. That is naturally true of its mechanisms as well, which—according to the setting—make the motor start to roll or unroll the fabric.

Planting at the Pond

After building the garden is almost finished and the land is securely walled in, the pond can finally be flooded. As the water level in the pond rises, the time for planting comes. First in line are the water lilies. Concrete rings of the right size were already set for the three different kinds of plantings when the pond was laid out.

On hot summer days, being on the southern terrace is pleasant only with sun protection. The attachment of a marquee is on schedule for shortly after the pond construction.

Instead of cold concrete plates, wooden planks are planned as sitting surfaces at the edge of the pond. The weather tight Douglas firm planks are mounted on aluminum brackets. The airy attachment with sufficient distance from the water lengthens the life of the boards considerably. Narrow gaps between them promote ventilation and drying.

The water lilies are set in concrete rings. These shaped pieces, 50 cm deep, prevent the strong roots from spreading out in the pond. The rings must be set in about 60 cm deep, so the water lilies are safe from frost. After planting, covering the substratum with gravel prevents lime particles from floating off.

The water plants should form luxuriant stands. They need a nutritious substratum made of mixed sand and lime soil. The shrubs, available in pots in garden centers, find their places in small groups in the shallow water zone. After the plants are divided, beds are opened in the gravel layer. After they are filled with substratum, the planting is done. Afterward the beds are covered with gravel again.

So these plants with their floating leaves can develop fully and bring forth a wealth of leaves and flowers in the next few years, they are given a nutritious substratum of lime and sand. The chunks of lime have already been broken up and mixed with building sand. After filling the substratum into the concrete rings, the water lilies can be planted in their places. With a rising water level, the chunks of lime dissolve, so that the roots are firmly enclosed in the substratum. To stop lime particles from floating away, the substratum is covered with gravel. The other pond plants similarly take suitable places in the vegetation zone. A few shovels of lime-sand mixture suffice for each plant. After moving the gravel aside, small piles of soil are made on the ground at the plant locations. On the shore a small Japanese maple is given a place in the gravel bed. Only after the growth and development of the water plants will additional ones be added in the water and on the shore.

Installing Edging Boards

To finish the swimming pool, only the attachment of edging boards is necessary. After cutting the boards out of weather-resistant Douglas fir and preparing aluminum brackets, they can be mounted on the concrete wall.

Finally, after weeks of work, the first swim is on the schedule. The body of water by the house door now invites swimming on nice days.

A BODY OF WATER FOR WADING FUN

An Open-Air Pond by the House Door

Combine Wading Pool with Biotope

On hot summer days a wading pool in your own garden always offers the chance to refresh yourselves. The children do not have to go a long way to the nearest lake or swimming pool, but can reach their open-air pool just a few steps across the terrace.

Above: Wading fun in your own pool. The water comes from the well and warms up in the sun.

To be sure, building a pool is only appropriate when all the children can swim and no small children are endangered anymore. Until then, the pond bed already in place can be used as a sandbox, or excavating the soil can wait to be done when the process of pond construction is ready to begin.

Naturally, a small pond also has something to offer adults, even if only a shallow wading bay is included. This is suitable, for example, as a Kneipp basin or for refreshing your legs.

But sitting by the water is also refreshing, especially if the pond is supplied by a bubbling spring. Just looking out the window and seeing this body of water by the house is a pleasure, especially on sunny summer days when the water surface has a silvery sheen and the songbirds quench their thirst. Even in winter, the pond by the door has a value as a place for the children to play. With lasting frost, a thick layer of ice forms and invites ice-skating. Of course no fish can rest in the depths of the water then. Otherwise they would be frightened. A wading pool should have a luxuriant plant zone. Reeds, rushes, and especially underwater plants like pondweed (*Elodea*) and parrot feather (*Myriophyllum*) contribute to filtering and supplying oxygen. Naturally, water lilies, iris, and other decorative plants may spread out, serving less to clear than to form the water garden.

Excavating and Shaping the Pond Bed

A small wading pool has enough room, even in a row-house garden—or as here, in a corner of the garden right by the house. A richly varied layout results, as a multi-level pond bed is uncovered. A spring with granite boulders contributes to it, taking form even as the soil work goes on. A shallow ditch from the spring to the pond forms the basis of a short brook bed. The high and low spots of the pond are dug out as planned. Depending on their positions, they serve as wading pools or plant zones. In laying out the pond, it should be remembered that sensitive plants need a sheltered place to develop unhindered. The constant stress from people using the pond, for example, is too much for water lilies. The plant zones off to the sides also give the animals in the pond a place of refuge.

Padding with Sand and Fleece

Constant use requires a protective substructure of foil. Besides special pond foils 1.5 mm thick, other plastics can also be had. The largest surface is covered by acrylic-fiber fleece. At the edges or at stones, slabs, perhaps left over from building the house, are also useful for padding.

Above: After the soil work, which was laboriously completed with a combination of elbow grease and a wheelbarrow, the pond bed is ready to be built up.

Below: The fleece precisely fits the shapes of the pond bed. The projecting edges are trimmed off with shears later.

Below: Along with the plastics, mineral building materials are used. A dry mortar offers the basis for setting border stones.

Here a drainpipe beside the house could be tapped. The overflow here is invisible under the porch floor.
An easily reached place is preferable for maintenance.

Avoiding Water Damage

In the planning process, possible problems inherent in a body of water should not be neglected. Holes in the foil or flooding from heavy rain must not damage the house. For such cases, well-functioning drainage or a spillway for overflowing—such as into a cistern—should be installed. For example, a spillway can be built at the lowest point on the bank, or a connection to an existing drainpipe can be made.

---

* **Building a Spillway**
Particularly in a situation near a house, building damage must be ruled out. To avoid water damage under heavy rain, a runoff to a household drainage system was built.

Laying Foil

As soon as the pond bed is padded and the necessary attachments are in place, it is time to lay the pond foil. As a rule, this is rolled by the supplier or folded according to a pattern. Spreading it must be done systematically, by plan, if there is one. Big heavy foils can be brought into the pond bed only with difficulty. Damage, such as by sharp stones or other sharp angles, must be avoided.

Spreading the tough foil goes better in warm than in cold weather.

The foil builds a watertight base for the further construction. It must be done from inside to outside to avoid tension on the foil.

*Attaching Foil
The water level is determined by the lowest spot on the banks; here this is under the porch. The foil must go right around the runoff pipe so no water can trickle through and damage the house.

The slightly leaning wall of granite blocks is bonded to the foil with mortar. The fleece padding absorbs the pressure.

The ladder must be attached firmly, so it will be steady for playing later.

Building a Wall

Steep walls are normally to be avoided when building a pond, as in such places it is not possible to cover the foil with gravel. But the deep-water area of a swimming pool can be enlarged by steep edges. The foil can then be protected by building a lattice of wood or a massive stone wall.

Installing a Ladder

So everybody can get into and out of the water easily, a ladder is installed. A homemade larch ladder must always be attached safely. For this reason it is given a concrete socket as soon as the right position is chosen. A flat granite stone serves as a steppingstone.

Filling the Pond

Such unusual prototypes are always experiments, so it is good to proceed slowly and with caution, watching for possible weak spots or evaluating and, if possible, improving them. In the course of excavation, tests of watertightness can be made at times. To do this, the pond is partly filled and the water level checked after a suitable time span. Repairs to the foil are extremely unpleasant and hard to make at this point. Special care in building is thus the best protection of the foil. Later it lies completely safe under the walls or gravel.

Left: The wading pool already stands out clearly in the pond. A balanced beam forms the border with the water-plant section.

Lower left: Planting can be done during the flooding. Here the water lilies are taking their places.

Below: During flooding, small particles come loose from the gravel. Later they will sink to the bottom.

Above: The water source naturally needs power. A pump does the job, pushing the water through a hose to the fountain stone.

Right: After the test, the hose disappears under the gravel. The hose diameter and height of the water source must suit the pump's capability.

* Natural Stone—a Formative Element

A bed of gravel should border the pond. The bright natural stone enlarges the area of the water garden. So the bed does not get overgrown, the gravel is spread on fleece. The bed of gravel also provides a path to the water.

A water garden is never completely finished—but its maintenance needs are limited.

*Various Stones

Even boulders can be uses as sitting stones and add to the shore formation; such chunks of stone are sometimes found during excavation. Large gravel can be had from contractors or gravel pits. Broken pieces of stone can also be used.

*The Water Test Provides Safety

Before swimming, it is good to know what qualities the water has. Various test sets can be had in the trade. With them, one can test the oxygen content, pH value, and other qualities by simple means. Here the color table shows a high pH value. This is very practical, as rainwater is usually neutral. (See the pond care chapter.)

BUILDING PONDS WITH HARD PLASTIC
Installing a Readymade Pool

Along with lime, concrete, and foil, hard plastic can be used to build a pond. The readymade pools of polyester or polystyrene have good and bad qualities compared with other pond-building materials.

They are very rigid, stable, withstand light and decay, and are completely watertight. But they must be installed properly, for bends or creases often result in cracks. Of course, such rigid pools are not flexible, meaning that their form is set. Their prices are also high. A small pool with 3 mm diameter, 80 cm depth, and about 2 cubic meter capacity can scarcely be had for less than 500 Euro.

So that a plastic pool gives long-term pleasure, careful installation is required. The basin must be sunk into the ground without twisting. There cannot be any hollow chambers beneath the basin. The walls must make contact with the ground everywhere. Otherwise the water pressure will cause distortions that in time will result in cracks or breaks. The more varied the shape and the larger the pool, the more difficult is the installation. The selected basin is usually delivered free, as transporting a large pool by car is scarcely possible.

Installing a Small Pool

On the site, a small plastic pool can easily be carried to the chosen spot by two people. When it is placed correctly, the outline is marked. This is simple to do with a round, rectangular or square pool by turning the basin upside down and marking its shape on the ground with sand. With an asymmetrical design, it is necessary to mark the outline with pegs. Then the pond bed can be excavated accordingly. The pool is set aside for the time being and the ground or lawn is removed from the marked surface as deep as the shallow-water level. This is about a spade deep. Then the pool is placed on the surface again and pressed down to the deep-water zone. This goes very well if one first gets in carefully and uses his own weight. The pool is immediately removed again and the soil dug out to the right depth on the marked surface. A stony soil needs to be dug out somewhat deeper than otherwise, so a thin layer of sand can be filled in as padding. So the pond bed fits properly and the pool is seated right, it must be fitted now and then. By impressions left behind when pressure is applied, it can be seen where more digging is necessary. Finally the pool is put permanently in place and the edges filled in with sand, so it has ground contact everywhere.

At the same time it is filled with water to prevent floating. Everything else, including planting and shore formation, will be no problem.

Soil Work by Machine

If a mini-excavator, or even a large excavator, is available after the house is built, it is simpler to dig out a large pit. As soon as the needed depth is reached, the ground is covered with sand for padding. So that the pool basin sits exactly level in the bed, the sand layer is smoothed with a level. Then the pool can be set in the prepared pit. Before filling in the excavated soil, it is necessary to fill the pool at least partly with water. Thus it remains firmly on the ground during the soil work. Especially when the soil is mixed with water it must already be flooded. Otherwise it will float like a boat and tip to the side.

Combining

Compared to pond foil, hard plastic basins are considerably more costly. If a large water garden is wanted, you can also form it with both materials. The plastic basin then serves as, for example, a central basin with a fountain. All around it a biotope with plants can be created on the foil.

Wood or Concrete Frames Covered with Foil

Alternatives of wood and pond foil have proved to be quite stable and watertight. A frame is built of planks or boards. This forms the shape when covered with pond foil. Similarly, concrete rings can be turned into stable water holes. Such basins are especially suitable for high bodies of water. They are simple to reach and take care of, just like high flowerbeds. If several basins are grouped, extensive bodies of water result.

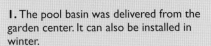

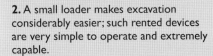

1. The pool basin was delivered from the garden center. It can also be installed in winter.

2. A small loader makes excavation considerably easier; such rented devices are very simple to operate and extremely capable.

3. A layer of sand on the bottom helps to even out and pad the bottom for the basin. The bottom is made horizontal with a level.

4. After sinking the plastic basin on the prepared pit, the mini-excavator fills in the soil. Flooding the pool with water prevents twisting.

5. After filling in the soil, the basin is solidly bedded in the ground. Meanwhile the gravel has also been filled in, to remain for some years as protection against accidents.

MAKING PONDS AND WELLS SAFE
Safety Devices on Bodies of Water

Plan, and Make It Real Afterward

Bodies of water can be dangerous, as they are a tremendous attraction for children. As long as the children cannot swim or underestimate the dangers that a well or pond contains, it is better to do without such bodies of water, or make them inaccessible.

If small children are part of the family (or are expected) during the garden planning and building, a pond should be ruled out. Of course, one can be included in the plans, as a pond brightens up and beautifies the garden, but it is better to postpone the building until the children are big enough. Until then, a lawn or flowerbed can be planted on the intended site.

Making an Existing Pond Safe

If a pond already exists in the garden—such as when one buys a house with a garden—or when children are born after the pond is built, it is imperative to immediately prevent danger there. For the effect of the sparkling waters on small children is powerful, and at the crawling age, even the shallowest basin can be dangerous. It is not enough to hold the children back, for it is scarcely possible over an extended period. The dangerous place can be made safe only by an effective barrier, unless one lets the water out and empties the basin.

Sand Instead of Water

A foil pond cannot be turned into a sandbox. But with a concrete or polyester basin, it is quite possible. Then the pond can be drained and filled with sand. The plants can be placed in a small basin off to the side, or in pots. Thus the pond becomes a completely danger-free, welcome playscape. For protection against rain or mud, a screen or roof of linen or plastic can be useful. Later, when there is no longer any danger, the sand is easy to remove and the basin can be turned into a pond again. Otherwise the pond could turn into a heath bed or a rhododendron garden if it were filled not with sand but with humus or some other appropriate substratum. But this option is better for the children than for the garden as a whole.

Pond Enclosure

Pond foil would also bear a covering of sand. Of course, pointed objects can damage the foil. In addition, while sand can easily be removed from a concrete or plastic basin, this requires special caution with a foil pond. Here only a secure enclosure, or even removal, becomes the last possibility. Before a foil pond is drained, dug out, and removed—which usually results in the loss of many plants and animals, and probably also the damaging and ruining of the foil—one might, for good or ill, prefer to erect a fence or covering in the bargain. Such a structure to ensure safety is not scenic, but safety comes first! A large-scale pond enclosure, including the area around it, is least conspicuous. This, of course, takes away much of the children's freedom of movement. Thus, a large-scale enclosure is only worthwhile when the pond lies off to the side and the size of the property allows for the loss of the area, meaning that enough free space remains. In a typical garden plot, a large-scale enclosure is scarcely possible. Here the pond has to be enclosed or covered directly. The enclosure must be sturdy, high enough, and thick. As a rule, a readily available fence of wire or wood, attached to well-anchored posts, is best suited. The fence is, of course, not a permanent structure and should be removable and usable elsewhere after a few years. When the posts or poles are driven in, naturally the foil must not be damaged. A certain distance from the water is necessary anyway, since the plants on the shore belong to the pond and should not be closed out. Access to the pond by means of a door is also important, so that maintenance can still go on. So that small animals can still reach the water, there must be a small gap between the fence and the ground. It cannot, though, be big enough for a child to slip through.

A Pond Behind Bars

It scarcely pays to fence in a small body of water, as it can be secured more easily with a grid. The grid of wood or metal mesh is laid on fixed points (such as

Steel grids put on for safety's sake must lie properly.

97

concrete rings) and kept horizontal. Here too, there must be no holes for children to slip through. The grid must have a small enough mesh and be immobile. But the water or shore cannot be closed to the animals. Naturally, this securing of the pond must be strong enough to hold a person's weight, even after some years. The grid must be appropriately impregnated or built of a non-decaying material.

Don't Build Traps

Nets or similar webbings are completely unsuitable. They give way and sink into the water. Whoever gets caught in one is even worse off than without this "safety" element. Grids with large gaps are also unsuitable.

Make it a principle to make sure that your pond securing is really safe and not a trap—for humans or for animals either!

A Pond in Winter

A surface of ice is just as fascinating as water. However, that icy surface forms a particular danger if it is thought to be hard and fit to walk on but only forms a thin covering. It must be absolutely assured that neither man nor beast will break through it, even in fairly shallow water. It should be made clear that walking on garden pond ice is dangerous for the fish and other pond life resting under it, since they do withdraw under ice for their own safety.

A covering of ice will not hurt the flora and fauna in the pond if it is about 60 cm deep. The animals rest under the ice and should not be disturbed.

Covering a Well

While a typical garden pond is dangerous only to children, a deep well or cistern can also become a trap for adults. Thus these sources of water should always be well secured, preferably with a massive cover of concrete, wood or metal. It must be strong enough to stand on and inflexible. A wooden lid needs to be waterproofed, for the constant evaporation will hasten rotting. A rotting lid must quickly be replaced by a new one. A good covering of metal can, for example, be a forged iron grid or a plate of rippled sheet metal. Galvanizing or waterproof paint protects this metal lid from rust. Concrete lids can be had in the trade in various sizes that fit the available concrete rings used for wells. They are very heavy, and children can hardly ever open them. Wooden or metal lids, in any case, need a lock, for they are rather ineffective otherwise. A ladder belongs in a well, unless it is fitted with climbing irons, which are often cast into concrete well rings. The ladder allows maintenance and checking of the well and is the last means of rescue if someone falls into the well. It must be free of rust and rot and well fastened, so that nobody can remove it.

Securing Other Bodies of Water

Even small water basins can be dangerous and should also be secured. Small basins—especially those with steep walls—are less dangerous for people than for animals, especially hedgehogs, mice, and other small animals. The basin lures a creature to drink—which is no danger if it is brim-full. With low water, though, animals easily fall in and cannot get out. Such basins need securing or a means of exit, perhaps small boards or a stone that serves as a bridge. This also applies to ponds with steep banks. There must be level passages from the water to the bank at least here and there.

A massive wooden lid secures the well and also offers a place for potted plants.

Swimming Pools

While a fall into an ordinary garden pond often causes no harm, an unwanted plunge into a swimming pool can have bad results. Such deep bodies of water must in any case be secured, perhaps by optimal lighting at night or by a sliding roof, so that nobody falls in—even in winter, when they are empty!

WATER FOR BALCONIES AND TERRACES
Tubs, Bowls, and Other Watertight Containers

Mini-Ponds

Bodies of water are valuable formative elements in any garden. They allow the growing of special plants and improve the local climate. Even on balconies and terraces, small water gardens can be laid out. Bowls and buckets do the job.

Ponds are taboo for families with small children—at least as long as they cannot swim. Bodies of water are like magnets to the little ones. They always present dangers if the children are not under control. However, making a small water garden is possible. Naturally, such mini-ponds can be located near the house, even when a large pond is close at hand. Such basins certainly have their charms. They can be grouped with potted plants or they may stand alone. A small pump brings motion into the water garden. The power—depending on the type—can come from an electric plug or a solar panel. The splashing is very refreshing on hot summer

As long as they have constantly damp roots, water plants can grow in flowerpots.

days. The price of the electricity stays within bounds, since a ten-watt pump delivers a strong spray. The containers for the waters must naturally be watertight for a long time. Mustered-out drink barrels made of wood, occasionally available in the trade, can be used. If necessary, they are given a watertight coating of thin pond foil or paint. Plastic containers (such as mortar tubs) wrapped in straw or otherwise covered are just as good. So are plastic containers nestled in appropriate clay pots and then covered with gravel. The best plants for them are those from native waters, but they must not be taken from natural ponds and lakes. It is better to buy young plants at the garden center or get them from your own garden pond. A few examples of selected types will suffice. Winter-resistant plants such as marsh marigolds, swamp iris, and calamus are ideal, as they can withstand a full freezing without harm. Plants like water hyacinths, shell flowers, and water ferns are not impervious to winter but survive the cold season in a cool winter garden. In the autumn one simply switches the flowerpots. Placing the pots on wooden laths and rollers makes them mobile. One can make such aids oneself.

Water Evaporates

On hot summer days the mini-ponds "consume" a lot of water. Rainwater can be used to refill them, either from a collector via a hose, or from a water barrel.

Your Own Water

Collecting Rainwater, Locating Ground Water

Every drop of rainwater that overflows and disappears is a loss. The plants bear the soft rainwater better than the often-hard water from the public pipes. It is beneficial to collect rainwater. This can be done in an ordinary barrel, or in a cistern built or buried near the house.

USING RAINWATER

Good Water From Above

Supplying Yourself

Rain supplies garden plants throughout the year; natural precipitation suffices for typical plants because the ground stores water. But it pays to collect rainwater for dry spells.

With the connection to the public water supply, many private wells and cisterns were abandoned. Now as then, it is much simpler to turn on the faucet than to carry water or pump it up. Yet the rainwater containers and ground-water wells are experiencing a renaissance for ecological reasons and because of the high cost of tap water. The household water collectors that may be purchased at reasonable prices also encourage this development. These capable pumps that turn on and off automatically supply the stored rainwater and make the use of watering devices or pond systems possible.

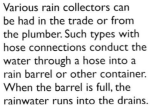

Various rain collectors can be had in the trade or from the plumber. Such types with hose connections conduct the water through a hose into a rain barrel or other container. When the barrel is full, the rainwater runs into the drains.

In the same way, rainwater from the collector, or after the rain barrel has been filled, can be conducted to the pond. The hose can also be buried underground.

BUILDING CISTERNS
Storing Water

Saving at the Right Time

Building a cistern can be done while the house is being built, after the soil has been dug out. Large concrete containers can be set in the ground near the house foundation. A crane truck delivers the container to the building site and lifts it to the prepared place. Setting a cistern in the foundation hole avoids later excavation or digging by hand. Special plastic tanks can also be had in the trade and buried in the ground.

Building a Cistern Later

When the house is standing and the garden is laid out, an underground water collector can still be built. A hole is dug at a favorable place—such as by a rain drainpipe. It must be the right size for the chosen container. Instead of a big concrete cistern or a plastic tank, concrete rings can also be placed in the hole, one atop another, to build a cistern. The rings from the building trade are 50 cm high; they have interior diameters of 100, 120, 150, 200 cm and other sizes. For 200 cm rings the hole must be some 250 cm wide, so the rings can be lowered by crane. For their delivery, a clear approach to the site must be available. Power lines must not be disturbed by the unloading. Digging by hand is only possible for small rings with diameters of about 100 cm. These concrete parts are extremely heavy. If no approach to the garden is available, the rings can be rolled to the building site. But this laborious transport technique is only possible on flat land. Then the rings have to be set into the hole. They may break in the process. Thus delivery by truck is always the best means of transport.

The thick walls of a concrete cistern with a cover on top are seen here. Such water collectors are extremely stable.

Plastic cisterns can be sunk in the garden afterward. Then only the top of the spout is seen above ground.

At a favorable location—such as beside a garden pond—a hole is dug. The excavated soil is useful elsewhere.

The big rings hold a lot of water that would otherwise go into the drains. It can be used to supply the pond.

After the ground is leveled, the concrete for a suitable baseplate is laid. For a cistern with a bottom, this is naturally not necessary.

After the crane has lowered the shaft rings into the hole, soil is filled in if possible. If necessary, the rings can be shifted slightly with an auto jack.

Covering the inside walls with waterproofing makes the concrete walls completely watertight. The fluid material can be spread with, for example, a paint roller.

Water can be removed by a jet pump, which is kept in a pump housing. A heavy cover is necessary for safety.

A test shows that the pump works. The water can be conveyed to the garden through a hose.

The water can also be moved by a hand pump, which also adds to the decoration of the cistern setup.

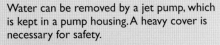

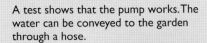

WELLS INSTEAD OF CISTERNS

Finding Ground Water

Natural Water Supply

When ground water is struck while the cellar hole is dug, a well can be built instead of a cistern.

Then it is worth digging some 50 cm deep into the ground water, so that the bottom ring is in the water. Usually such a well supplies water as long as water from the environment trickles through. In this case one need only set the other rings atop the bottom one and cover the well with a lid, or build a wellhead.

Survey the Market]

The building materials market offers various devices and components for gathering and dispensing water. Along with large plastic tanks that can be buried in the garden, there are rain barrels in various sizes that can be placed right under the drainpipes of the house. These plastic barrels also offer a large storing potential if several of them are used together and connected by hoses.

Tapping Drainpipes

Large cisterns buried in the garden are connected with the drainpipes from the roof after being installed. A runoff connected with the drains is not to be forgotten. Small rain cisterns that are built or set up later can be fitted with special rain collectors. Such devices with hose connections or opening tops can be had in the trade. Installation is possible at any time. Often the drainpipes on the house are prepared for it. They only need to be detached, which is easy to do using wing nuts. After a piece of drainpipe is removed, the cistern is simply set in place.

> *** Obey Local Regulations**
> Before tapping ground water with a well, inquire at the appropriate local office. Sometimes there are limitations on the use of ground water for reasons of water rights or hygiene.

A rain collector with a lid makes the water available when the lid is removed. Otherwise it runs out into the drains.

A pond can be directly useful in collecting rainwater if it is built right beside the house. The water then runs from the roof directly into the pond without detours.

Building a Brook
Running Water

Water only has an effect when it moves. A splashing brook livens up any garden. It can be a short cascade or a long stream.

When building a brook, one should place special emphasis on the proper surroundings. So the water does not run "sluggishly", dams are needed. When building with finished elements, bubbling passages come into being anyway. The parts are stacked up so that they overlap. Then the water has to flow from one element to the next and finally into the pond. The finished parts of plain or sanded plastic or special artificial stone elements are expensive, though. A homemade brook can be just as effective—if it is built properly. Only pieces of pond foil (such as leftovers from the pond) and angled stones and gravel are needed.

RUNNING WATER
A Brook on a Slope

Using Natural Slopes

At first the course is determined. A shallow ditch suffices as a brook bed. Only small quantities of water will flow through it. But if this is to be effective, the bed must be dug out properly. As a rule, the work begins at the mouth to the pond.

So that it splashes properly here, a substructure, perhaps with a concrete slab, is a good idea. The piece of foil then falls almost vertically away to the mouth. So that the water does not run off to the right and left, the foil edges are raised and properly built up. A test with a hose and pump shows whether the water runs right. In this way the brook bed is built up to the highest point. This can be, for example, a bored-out spring stone or a millstone. Between the source and the mouth there are several steps, each formed with angled stones on the substructure. Small collecting pools, in which the water stops during its flow, are made. As soon as the brook bed is covered with foil, the water should flow steadily. If not, changes should be made. The final buildup with gravel covers only the foil. The hose from the pump to the source can simply be buried in the ground beside the brook. It is dug in only when the water runs right.

An alternative to a babbling brook is a bubbling spring that gives the same acoustic effect. It can be a spring fountain or a water pipe placed at the right height.

Suitable Pumps

Naturally, the spring only bubbles properly if it has the right pump. It must be suited to the overall height to be surmounted from the water level in the mouth basin to the spring stone. The diameter of the hose must be taken into account, as must the desired strength of the spray. A simple immersion pump or drainage pump is best suited for brook use. Such pumps can be had for about 50 Euro. For example, a 300-watt pump as a maximum pumping height of some six meters and a maximum pumping power of 8000 liters per hour, or 130 liters per minute. The quantity decreases as the height increases. With a height of, for example, two meters, a 30-watt immersion pump still supplies 7000 liters of water. This suffices for a strong fountain and a running brook. Naturally, a solar system would be ideal for running a brook. But this would require a capable module and a strong pump.

Direct-Current Pumps

Special systems for running a brook are available at garden shops. They function reliably after installation and need little electricity, as the pumps run on only 40 watts and yet have a high level of effect. Direct-current pumps are also available and are especially suitable for swimming or wading pools (see Wading Pools for Children). There is no danger from them if the electric cable is damaged.

Step-by-step Brook Building

1. A slope offers a site for the brook. The rough work at the mouth is easier with a mini-excavator. Forming the bed is handwork. For a frost-free pond depth of 60 cm, the bed has to be dug out correspondingly deeper for the sand padding.

2. The upper pond is already finished and serves as a source of water for the brook. The water level here depends on its spillway to the brook. Before trimming the foil, the brook has to be set up. If necessary, the foil can still be under-filled if the water level is too low.

3. A shallow ditch dug in the slope suffices for the brook. Forming of small ponds and curves brings variety to its course. The foil will later fit snugly into the shaped course of the brook. Here too, filling in can be done when the foil is already spread out in the bed.

4. The spillway from the source pond to the brook bed requires special care. The foil in the bed must be attached very firmly to the rim of the pond. This is done by overlapping the pond and brook foil. A special adhesive band can be added for watertightness.

5. Laying the foil piece by piece makes it possible to build the brook with scraps from the pond edges. Short pieces can also be laid more easily than long ones. But they have to be stuck together to make them watertight, or overlapped so no water trickles through.

6. So no water runs out on the edges, filling in with excavated soil is necessary. In this way the foil is laid in the brook bed from the top down. But the foil edges also can be placed and filled in below as soon as the water runs. Thus the foil should be measured large and project over the edges.

7. While laying out the foil pieces, building with stones is also done. Round pieces that give the water garden a mountainous character work best.

8. The falls and course of the brook depend on the angle and height of the slope. Flat areas with ponds and falls dug into the slope afford variety.

9. Along with the brook building is the construction of the mouth. While the water is running, distribute the gravel, fill in piles of substrata, and set plants in.

10. A piston pump sunk in the pond pumps the water through a hose up to the source pond. When the water is already running while the brook bed is being built, it is easy to see where the stones should be placed.

11. So the water does not run off under the stones but splashes down over them effectively, every stone has to be placed carefully.

12. The water is already running right; now the work goes on, stone by stone. Parallel to it, the future water garden can be completed by planting trees and shrubs.

13. A systematic construction is worthwhile, as the brook contributes to the garden formation when it is finished. The time-consuming work avoids later improvements and repairs to the foil.

14. At the finished stretches of the brook, the foil can already be trimmed off neatly. Making the edges high and piling up gravel forms a border for the bordering plants.

15. The "mountain brook" slowly takes its final form. Small gravel has already been spread on the foil among the stones.

16. The pond has also taken on its final form. Here too, the foil is trimmed off neatly when the shore formation has been finished.

17. The shore plants have grown well, and the first water lilies are spreading out in the pond. Nothing more can be seen of the pond foil.

PLANTS IN AND BY THE WATER

Plants in and by the Water

Selected Trees and Shrubs

In nature, bodies of water do not stay bare long. Willows and alders find homes on the shores, and floating and submerged plants soon grow in the water. Seeds and plant parts that put out roots even in nutrient-poor gravel turn the place green. Of course lakes, rivers, and fishponds offer more room for natural spreading than the usual home garden. Here willows can scarcely grow, or only a few of them, perhaps pollard trees that are kept small by pruning. Small types, such as pussy willows, even find enough root space in large pots. Before planting, it should be remembered that native plants are particularly likely to thrive.

SWIMMERS, DIVERS, ETC.

Planting Water Plants Purposefully

Thriving Plants with an Urge to Spread

Make your choices deliberately, and remember the saying, "fewer plants develop better than too many". To be sure, there are also possibilities of limiting them to pots or baskets, so that plant-friends can plant many desired types and their joy in a water garden will not be too troubled.

Above: Water hyacinth
(*Eichhornia*)

Left: Water lily (*Nymphaea*)

Page 116: Tropical water lily
(*Nymphaea* 'Dr. Moore')

Page 117: White water lily
(*Nymphaea alba*)

When you want to use plants to clear a swimming pool or rainwater collecting basin, you can plant it luxuriantly. In a clearing pond you can even let reeds and rush grasses spread. A small decorative pool by the terrace, of course, offers space only for a chosen few types. Water lilies can have a place here, as they rank, now as then, among the loveliest water plants. Naturally, fans of rare or exotic plants know what they are taking in the bargain in terms of special care. Even lotuses and water hyacinths grow in our latitudes—and must naturally come inside in the winter.

Most water plants, such as water lilies, swamp iris and marsh marigolds and perennials, are lasting flowers that constantly spread. There are also woody shore plants like willows or alders that are long-lived. While trees stay in one place and form the crown or bush that is typical of their kind, most spreading flowers grow from root runners. Where reeds, rushes, and purple loosestrife find places to spread, they fill them sooner or later, and thoroughly! Such plants, which spread from strong runners, thus should grow only in large water gardens or be limited from the very start. Otherwise they will overwhelm less hardy plants and fill a small pond completely in just a few years. Where this is wanted in a clearing basin, naturally it is quite all right. In a small water-lily pond in a row-house garden, such plants make more work than joy. Here only selected species may grow. Special caution is urged for the deliberate growing of such neophytes. The best known of them include giant hogweed or bear's-claw (*Heracleum mantegazzianum*) and Himalayan balsam (*Impatiens glandulifera*). They have settled on native riverbanks and form thick stands in places.

Above: Swamp iris (*Iris pseudacorus*)

Left: Bog bean (*Menyanthes trifoliate*)

Left center: Marsh marigold (*Caltha palustris*)

Right center: Water lily, etc. (*Nymphaea*)

Bottom: Canadian pondweed (*Elodea canadensis*)

* **Algae Need Light to Grow**
Sunny warm bodies of water encourage the development of algae. Forming algae in a pond can be decreased markedly by shading, such as with swimming-leaf plants.

PLANTING BY THE WATER
Planting Banks and Edges

Planting Trees and Shrubs

A water garden does not live only from the wet zone, but also considerably from the green belt. So it may gladly spread from the shore. The size of the water surface and the shore zones around it are influenced by the selected types of plants.

Left: Primroses *(Primula rosea)*

Right: Dwarf willow with swamp plants

The more plants are supposed to grow in a water garden, the more space has to be cleared for them. Invasive types like reeds, rushes, and bamboo reed spread more strongly than small plants like water plantain, arrowhead, and pygmy rush. They move into the background or stay away entirely when they could disturb permanently. If necessary—as in a small pond—invasive species are put in a corset of plastic or concrete, so that other plants do not disappear in the thick growth. A borderline is also possible in the form of a separate body of water. In a basin of their own, separated from the pond, reed-mace and rushes can spread out in peace. There they can serve, for example, as effective rainwater filters. They do not then take any space away in the main pond, and they leave more living space for the less invasive plants to expand.

Many Different Kinds

Water plants divide themselves in their occurrence into deep and shallow zones as well as in form and flower color. There are grassy ones with long slim leaves like reeds, rushes or calamus, bushy types like sedges, bur-reed, and club rush, creepers like meadow buttercup, marsh marigold,

and monkey flower, and naturally those types that spread underwater or float on the surface. They are essentially species that grow for some years and form more and more luxuriant stands. When planting them, not only must the right plant depths be maintained; the expansion and forms have to be considered all the more. Large plants like reeds and rushes belong in the background; small ones like marsh marigolds or monkey flowers are better in forward areas. Otherwise they will fade in time into the thicket of the invasive types. Flower colors can also be arranged deliberately. Yellow swamp iris will go well with red water lilies. The yellow skunk cabbage also combines well with rose-red primroses. The blue pickerelweed is very striking along with blue water hyacinths. Many other combinations are pleasantly noticeable. But always plant several examples of a species in small groups. Only then are the flower colors effective. To be sure, the flowers only last for a limited time. For that reason the color effect of the flowers should have a stronger effect. Evergreen types like horsetail or brooklime have their value particularly after the fullness of summer. But brown reeds and the seed heads of reed-mace are not to be despised in the winter.

Trees and Shrubs

Of course a water garden is not limited to the wet or damp zones. Shore areas as extensive as possible should belong to it. Thus the formative possibilities also expand considerably. With selected trees like dwarf or polled willows, and suitable flowering plants like purple loosestrife, which offers a richness of mauve flowers, and yellow loosestrife with its glowing yellow blossoms, the water garden can be made extremely varied and colorful. Whoever does not limit the array strictly to typical water and shore plants can naturally create much more. Larkspur, phlox, lupines, and a host of other flowering plants do not look lost beside the water. Flowering shrubs like forsythia, blossoming cherries, and weigelia also fit in. In principle, no objection can be made to any flowering plant if it is placed correctly. Even herbs like salvia and lavender can grow by the water, and whoever wants to can also plant decorative useful plants like artichokes, zucchini, rhubarb or corn by his pond. Annual summer flowers like marigolds, floss flowers or big sunflowers can make a season pleasantly noteworthy. Suitable locations should be found and the chosen flowers should be given sufficient space for the near future. Of course changes are not ruled out and always necessary.

Left: a flowerbed by the pond.

Center: Planting swamp iris.

Above: Various shore and water plants.

Below: Planting Japanese maple in a gravel bed.

VARIETY FOR INSIDE AND OUTSIDE
Plant List and Care Tips

Above: Iris (*Iris sibirica*)

Middle: Lotus (*Nelumbo lotus*)

Bottom: Water lettuce (*Pistia stratiotes*)

Plants that Grow in Water

Plant	Depth	Height	Blooms	Color
Marsh Marigold: *Caltha palustris*	0.10 cm	20 cm	spring	yellow, white
Water Velvet: *Azolla caroliniana*	floats	flat	--	--
Brooklime: *Veronica beccabunga*	0-50 cm or floats	creeps	summer	blue
Common Rush: *Juncus effuses*	0-50 cm	60 cm	summer	brownish
Flowering Rush: *Butomus umbellate*	5-30 cm	50 cm	summer	pink
Watercress: *Nasturtium officinale*	0-10 cm	30 cm	June	white
Bog Bean: *Menyanthes trifoliate*	0-20 cm	ca. 30 cm	May-June	white
Water plantain: *Alisma plantago-aquatica*	5-30 cm 100 cm	50 cm	summer	white flowers
Yellow Loosestrife: *Lysimachia sp.*	Shore or flat or 0-20 cm	50 cm	May-July	yellow
Buttercup: *Ranunculus sp.*	0-30 cm	flat or - 100 cm	summer	yellow, white
Pickerelweed: *Pontederia cordata*	0-30 cm	30 cm	summer	blue
Bur-Reed: *Sparganium sp.*	0-30 cm	30-60 cm	summer	white
Calamus: *Acarus calamus*	5-50 cm	70 cm	April-July	green
Water Soldiers: *Stratiotes aloides*	50 cm	floating	summer	white
Pondweed: *Potamogeton sp.*	50 cm on	underwater	summer	green
Lotus: *Nelumbo nucifera*	0-50 cm	200 cm	summer	white
Mint: *Mentha sp.*	Shore or 0-30 cm	50 cm	summer	blue
Arrowhead: *Sagittaria sp.*	0-20 cm	50 cm	summer	white
Reed-Mace: *Typha sp.*	0-50 cm	50-200 cm	summer	brown
Horsetail: *Equisetum sp.*	0-50 cm	50-100 cm	--	--
Skunk Cabbage: *Lysichiton sp.*	0-10 cm	30 cm	spring	white, yellow
Reed: *Phragmites australis*	0-50 cm	1-4 m	summer	whitish
Floating Fern: *Salvinia natans*	floating	flat	--	--
Water Snowflake: *Nymphoides sp.*	20-120 cm	floating	summer	yellow
Water Lily: *Nymphaea sp.*	30-100 cm	floating	summer	various
Club Rush: *Scirpus sp.*	0-50 cm	30-100 cm	summer	brown
Water Arum: *Calla palustris*	5-20 cm	20 cm	summer	white
Forget-me-not: *Myosotis sp.*	0-10 cm	30 cm	summer	white
Mare's Tail: *Hippuris vulgaris*	0-50 cm	ca.100 cm	--	--
Milfoil: *Myriophyllum sp.*	20 cm up	underwater	--	--
Spatterdock: *Nuphar lutea*	100 cm	floating	summer	yellow
Water Hawthorn: *Aponogeton distachyos*	50 cm	flat	summer	white
Featherfoil: *Hottonia palustris*	20 cm	underwater	spring	white
Water Hyacinth: *Eichhornia Crassipes*	floating	flat	summer	blue
Duckweed: *Lemna minor*	floating	flat	--	--
Water Chestnut: *Trapa natans*	floating	flat	summer	white
Canadian Pondweed: *Elodea Canadensis*	20 cm up	underwater	--	--

Plants that Grow in Water (continued)

Plant	Depth	Height	Blooms	Color
Water Lettuce: *Pistia stratiotes*	floating	flat	--	--
Bladderwort: *Utricularia sp.*	30-100 cm	underwater	summer	yellow
Swamp Iris: *Iris pseudacorus*	0-20 cm	100 cm	June	yellow
Cotton Grass: *Eriophorum sp.*	0-10 cm	30-50 cm	summer	white
Sedge: *Cyperus sp.*	10-20 cm	50-120 cm	summer	green, brown

** **Information and Notes**
Before making your choice, look around in botanical gardens or at garden shows.
Model water gardens are often to be seen there. On the basis of the name labels,
decide which flowers to order at garden shops and plant in your own garden.*

TREES	Height	Blooms
Angelica Tree: *Aralia elata*	2-3 m, sparse	yellowish in summer, big leaves
Serviceberry: *Amelanchier lamarckii*	3-5 m, bushy	white in April, red in autumn
Alder: *Alnus viridis*	1-3 m, bushy	insignificant
Pussy Willow: *Salix caprea pendula*	ca. 2-3 m, hanging	typical
Japanese Maple: *Acer palmatum*	3-5 m, fanlike	insignificant
Goat Willow: *Salix caprea*	ca. 3 m, bushy	yellow catkins in March-April
Swiss Willow: *Salix Helvetica*	ca. 0.50 m	silvery, in spring
Butterfly Bush: *Buddleia sp.*	2.3 m, loose, bushy	various, good nectar source
Dwarf Birch: *Betula humilis*	1-2 m, bushy	insignificant

FLOWERS	Height	Blooms
Purple Loosestrife: *Lythrum salicaria*	80-100 cm	violet-red, June to August
Lady's Mantle: *Alchemilla sp.*	30-50 cm	yellow, June-July
Hosta: *Hosta sp.*	30-60 cm	white, June-July
Monkey Flower: *Mimulus luteus*	30-50 cm	yellow, May to August
Yellow Loosestrife: *Lysimachia punctata*	50-80 cm	yellow, June to August
Ligularia: *Ligularia sp.*	100-200 cm	yellow, July to September
Meadowsweet: *Filipendula sp.*	50-100 cm	white or pink, June-July
Primrose: *Primula sp.*	20-50 cm	various colors, spring
Umbrella Plant: *Darmera/Peltiphyllum*	50-80 cm	pink, April-May
Day Lily: *Hemerocalis sp.*	50 cm	yellow, red, June to August
Joe-Pye-Weed: *Eupatorium sp.*	100-200 cm	mauve, July to September
Snakeweed: *Polygonum bistorta*	50-80 cm	pink, May to August

Above: Blutweiderich (*Lythrum salicaria*)

Below: Lgelkolben (*Sparganium*)

Animals in and by the Water

Flyers, Swimmers, and Divers

With the first casual glance at the pond, one sees strange animals. But whoever looks deeper into the water can make many a discovery. In the wet are tadpoles, salamanders, and moderlieschen (ray-finned fish). The first winged guests came while the garden pond was being built. Dragonflies seem to know that they will soon find water there. The big insects cannot be overlooked, but their larvae are scarcely seen. They live underwater and feed on tiny animals. Tadpoles assuage their hunger with mosquito larvae and other insects. As soon as they have developed, the voracious robbers pop up to shed their old skin. The empty shells are often found on water-lily stalks or other plants. The grown dragonflies prove to be skilled fliers. They can stop in the air and suddenly restart when they have spotted a victim or are themselves endangered. Along with the blue Widow Skimmer, the rare Pondhawk, and the magnificent Green Darner, there are many other species. A deliberate settlement in your own garden is scarcely possible. But a layout with as much variation as possible, with open areas of water and luxuriant greenery on the shore, does the job.

WILD AND TAME ANIMALS
Life with the Water

Many Kinds

Ponds that approach nature invite many animals. Diving beetles have proved to be effective little robbers in a pond. The big swimmers catch mosquito larvae. In a lifeless body of water—such as a rain barrel or a puddle—these burdensome little creatures have ideal conditions for development.

Above: Goldfish (*Carassius auratus*) become tame.

Upper right: Slow-worm (*Anguis fragilis*).

Lower right: mussels migrate on the bottom.

They gather in crowds just below the surface and dive lightning-fast when enemies approach. In a populated pond these insects have no chance. Here dragonfly larvae, water beetles, and other enemies are hunting them. If need be, the addition of fish can be helpful. Just one day after the addition of a few goldfish, nothing more of the mosquito brood can be seen. Thus, even fish are useful in a garden pond. But their use should be considered well, for the fish also catch other insects. In any case, enough moving space is necessary. The pond must also be deep enough to let the animals to descend into frost-free zones in winter. This is equally true of moderlieschen, yellow-wort, and other fish, as well as frogs, which overwinter either in holes in the ground, under piles of leaves on the shore, or in the water. At that time, these changeable amphibians breathe through their skin. Only in spring, when the sun warms the water, do they pop up again and become active. Frogs catch flies and other insects. They are very attached to their locality as long as the necessities of life are sufficient.

From the eggs of frogs, which they lay in spring, come a multitude of tadpoles. These "frog children" eat everything, including each other.

Toads come back to their birthplace every year to mate; the males wait for hours for the females. Take note of these creatures when you maintain your pond in the spring.

Above: The small water frog has spent the winter on the shore; the home-loving animals often settle in a garden on their own.

Right: Cats like to go fishing. These young ones are not very successful yet.

A Variety of Types

Water frogs—just like toads and other amphibians—not only need enough room to move around, but also protected places to rest. For example, they like wooden steps, sitting stones or other places by the water. Here they sit on sunny summer days and let the sun warm them. If danger comes, a jump into the water saves them. Salamanders that spend their lives primarily under water are less jumpy. These amphibians also have long lives. But like fish and frogs, they need a frost-free home in the water and hiding places in the pond. Biotopes with a variety of underwater plants offer ideal living conditions. Pondweeds and other plants that form luxuriant stands but do not overwhelm the water area are best. The vital underwater plants either swing freely (such as Canadian pondweed) and can be fished out easily if they spread too much, or they take root in the bottom of the pond. Here too, reducing them in the process of pond maintenance is easy, but these productive oxygen producers should thrive very well as they filter nutrients out of the water. Along with the useful plants, water fleas are also good for cleaning the water. The tiny crablike animals indicate a high water quality. Just like water fleas, water snails contribute to cleaning. Even ramshorn and spitzhorn snails feed on algae lawns. These worthy snails should be allowed to multiply. Then too, a goodly growth of algae should be allowed. Algae are evergreen plants and offer frogs hiding places in winter. In the spring, when they grow especially strongly, the thick bundles can simply be raked out and composted.

On hot days, dogs also like to take a dip. The dog cannot harm a hard plastic basin. Under the protection of gravel, pond foil is also protected from scratches and such.

AMPHIBIANS, REPTILES, INSECTS, ETC.

Permanent and Temporary Guests

The male White Corporal
(*Libellula exusta*)

Animals in and by the Water (selection)

Species	Life Style	Overwintering
Goldfish *Carassius auratus*	social, in groups, also with other types	resting in deep water or safe in the house
Orfe (or Ide) *Leuciscus idus*	social, in groups, faster than goldfish, only for larger ponds	resting in deep water
Edible Frog *Rana esculenta*	social, in water or on the shore	dug in on bank or pond bottom
Smooth Newt *Triturus vulgaris*	lone, only together for mating in water or on shore	dug in to hibernate
Ramshorn Snail *Planobarius corneus*	social, valuable algae eaters	underwater in frost-free zones
Common Toad *Bufo bufo*	lone, social for mating	dug in on the shore stays at one location
Sand Lizard *Lacerta agilis*	lone or paired in own territories	dug in on the bottom
Slow-Worm *Anguis fragilis*	actually a lizard (not a snake)	dug in on the bottom in moist biotopes
Grass Snake *Natrix natrix*	rare, in moist biotopes with rocks and rough land	in holes or dug in away from water
Dragonflies (many species)	lone, paired for mating	larvae in water or mud

Sounds in May—frogs croak with the help of sound chambers that they fill with air. Their nightly concerts are limited to the mating season in spring.

Pumps, Filters, Hoses, and Equipment

Pond Technology

A properly built, simple pond needs no special technical devices, such as filter pumps, water cleaners, aerators, and the like. Algae live on the bottom or form string-like bunches that can simply be fished out with a rake. As soon as the newly planted water plants have grown well and formed luxuriant stands, they contribute to the clearing and reducing of nutrients from the water. Unlike with simple decorative animals or biotopes, capable filters and the appropriate accessories may be needed in fishponds, especially if one is raising Koi. Naturally, technical devices do not need to be avoided in ordinary ponds, such as when a fountain stone or spring is desired. Such mobile water places must, of course, be correctly located, so the stream of water does not disturb water plants or damage leaves.

BRINGING WATER INTO MOTION

Select and Install the Right Equipment

Pumps to Meet Your Needs

Solar pumps that run on the sun's energy are most effective. They need no electric power from the plug and run reliably and service-free as long as they get enough sunlight. Solar pumps are also fully danger-free. There is no danger of a shock in case of a short circuit.

The performance of the module must be attuned to the pump. For a small solar pump, some 20 to 40 watts of power are needed. For a bigger pump, considerably more modules will be required. It is recommended that such a system be bought from a competent dealer who also assists in the installation or at least shows a similar system. If necessary, he may take back the pump and module or exchange them if they produce too little power. In terms of experience, solar pumps and modules function reliably for many years. The changed water volume in the switch between clouds and sunshine is not a problem. The more or less strong bubbling can even be pleasant. Besides, a solar pump with a module is an ideal source of alternative energy. The effect of the simple system that costs nothing to run can convince any visitor. The waterpower provided by solar energy is, of course, limited by the fact that the initial costs are, alas, still far above those of similar AC or DC systems that depend on the electric network. And solar modules can also be used for other purposes.

Pumps for a Brook

Naturally, the power of a small solar system is not enough to run a big fountain or a brook, as few modules can provide more than a modest height. For a strong flow in a brook bed or from a fountain, special pond pumps, available with different performances from different manufacturers, are needed. According to their type, they

DC pumps receive their power from a transformer. This power converter must be located where it is protected from moisture.

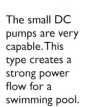

The small DC pumps are very capable. This type creates a strong power flow for a swimming pool.

The pump in the pond pushes the water through a hose to a fountain or brook source. The hose must be the right size and as invisible as possible under the gravel. Gravel also hides pond foil and covers the substratum in the plant baskets.

move 50 to 250 liters of water per minute (or 3000 to 15,000 liters per hour). The appropriate pump must be based on the water flow. Along with the amount of flow, the height difference between the pump's location in the pond and the fountain needs to be considered in particular. Then too, the hose has to be right for the pump. Old-style pumps are rotary types that do well with comparatively little power. A pump with 75 watts of power can move some 5500 liters of water to a height of 2.5 meters in an hour. In comparison, traditional piston pumps (immersion pumps), otherwise used

to move well water or remove dirty water, need some 300 watts of power for the same quantity of water.

Such piston pumps can create a height of more than five meters. The decision for a piston pump (common immersion pump) or a rotary pump (special pond pump) depends particularly on its functional range, or in brook building, the pumping height. Then too, solar pumps are also rotary pumps that produce waterpower by means of rotating propellers. The piston pumps work with a cylinder. Another type of pump, used especially for pumping water out of a well, is the garden or jet pump. Such pumps, that are often offered with a pressure equalizer and are portrayed as house waterworks, use some 1000 watts to produce a high pressure (ca. 5 bar). Thus they attain pumping heights of over 40 meters. To be sure, the quantity pumped, some 3000 liters per hour, is less than that of a piston or rotary pump. Garden pumps are suction pumps that stand dry.

Filters for a Water Garden

Just as a typical garden pond does not need a pump if no water play is wanted, neither does it need a filter. The water plants clean the water if enough different types are used (especially underwater plants like *Elodea* or *Myriophyllum*). In addition, the influx of fresh water helps to clear the pond, as much water evaporates in summer. Yet filters have a value, such as when many fish dirty the water with their droppings, or if a swimming pool is often used.

In using a pond pump, such as for a fountain or a brook, the pump can be set

Typical immersion pumps produce more pressure than average pond pumps. They are used to overcome a large height difference between the pond and source.

up without special effort. A pump-filter combination is the simplest to install. Such devices differ from pond pumps only by being equipped with a filter. Pond filters with pumps, like pond pumps, can be had in various sizes. External filters set in a shaft near the pond and run by a pump in the pond give higher performance. Such filters in round plastic containers can be used, for example, in small swimming pools or ponds with fish. Multi-chambered filters that are placed on the pond's shore as removable modular systems perform better. A suitable pond pump, installed in the water, is needed to operate them. Such large filters contain coarse filtering mats that retain coarse materials, plus a chamber with lava grains in which microorganisms settle, which disintegrate fine materials such as algae, manure, and the like. In a third chamber is a storage-capable granulate of natural stone, which binds poisonous materials. Such external filters, offered by several manufacturers in varying sizes and versions, must be readily accessible on the shore. Thus the filter media can be cleaned at any time. Make sure the suction pump and the outflow opening or hose from which the filtered water flows back into the pond are as far from each other as possible. Only then is an optimal circulation with good filtering action to be attained.

Pre-Filters for Multi-Chamber Filters

The effect of an external filter can even be improved by connecting a pre-filter. These small devices, also found in dealers' stocks as ultra-violet water clearers, take algae out of the water with the help of UV light; they are then removed by the main filter. In this way, green algae in the water can be avoided. Pre-filters also kill harmful bacteria and germs.

A solar pump creates a powerful spray. The modules must fit the pump and be turned toward the sun.

Surface Skimmers

Among the water filters are the so-called skimmers or surface suckers. Such pre-filters float just under the surface of the water and suck up leaves, floating algae, and other solid particles.

Hose and Accessories

Pond pumps, filters, and the like should be connected by spiral hose. This special stiffened hose—unlike the usual garden hose—cannot fold. They are stable in UV light and do not decay. There are also suitable lengthening hoses, connectors, separators, reducers, and other connecting elements needed for faultless installation.

Such filters hold solid particles back from the intake hose (such as when taking water from a cistern).

Pond Care

Care Depends on the System

Properly designed water gardens need less care than, for example, lawns. How much is determined by the owner and influenced by the type of layout. While a wet biotope off to the side can grow as undisturbed as possible, a swimming pool needs regular cleaning. The care also depends on the plants and the size. The bigger and more varied the water garden is, the easier it is to care for. Water plants always have enough room to spread, so that intervention to reduce them is rarely needed. Besides, a big pond had more water-storage capability. The rain replaces the evaporated water. Additional supplying with water is rarely necessary, if at all. In a big pond, sensitive water plants need less protection than in a small or shallow body of water. It hardly ever occurs that a big pond freezes to the bottom, which can happen to a small pond. And the quality of the system depends on the care.

A properly designed pond remains in good condition for years if it is situated in a good place and was built and planted with care.

CARE ALL YEAR ROUND
Purposeful Intervention in a Water Garden

Water quality has an essential
effect on the development of
a water garden. In a swimming pool in particular, the
waster should be tested now
and then. There are simple
test sets with which the pH
value, oxygen and nitrogen
contents, and other values
can be measured.

Maintaining and Renewing

A typical well-built garden pond with some 5 to 30 square meters of surface needs little care over the year to remain healthy, thriving, and scenic. Care is essentially limited to supplying it with fresh water, which can be supplied automatically by rainwater. In the spring in particular, the time of algae growth, these unwanted water plants can be simply raked out in large quantities. Dead plant parts, if any, can be removed with them. Cutting back wilted plants and grasses, though, must be done before the new growth. Reeds and rushes, or shore plants like lamplighter grass and others that die off above ground, should not be trimmed in the autumn. The tufts also look good in winter and provide shelter and seeds for animals. In the spring, before the fresh shoots appear from the roots, the wilted growths can be removed and the clumps trimmed with shears.

Minor replanting is also possible late in the winter, as is the increasing of water and

> *** Beware of Sharp Leaves**
> Be extra careful with Chinese reeds. The long leaves are sharp as knives and cause serious wounds if they slide through your hand while you trim them.

shore plants by separating. If necessary, trees on the shore can be pruned or disturbing branches can be cut. Early bloomers like pussy willows are better trimmed after they bloom. In the spring, as soon as no more frost will come, the overwintered exotic plants like water hyacinths or shellflowers can be brought out. In summer, the water garden—if necessary—gets fresh water. Swamp plants, of course, can only be supplied with calcium-free rainwater, which is also easy for all other pond plants to bear. But most of them also accept calcium-bearing tap water or spring water without harm, as long as it is always diluted by rainwater. Maintaining the water quality has a very decisive effect on the condition and development of water plants. Occasional tests with simple indicators show, among others, the contents of oxygen, carbon dioxide, and calcium, and other materials. Such tests are particularly useful if plants are suffering or sickening, and in any case before any treatment with chemical materials such as algae killers and the like. The failings are usually easy to spot and cure by simple means like adding fresh water. If small plants are obviously threatened by invasive types, this can be helped only by limiting or removing the root growths. Water plants rarely have to fight with harmful animals (such as plant lice) or diseases (like fungal infections). Sometimes, for example, borer moths attack the leaves of water lilies. They can be strongly reduced by

Getting a mini-lab for water testing pays as long as the test sets give precise data that foster safety. If necessary, for example, calcium-rich water can be neutralized by adding rainwater.

gathering the larvae or picking off attacked leaves without using chemical means. This is also true of other animal pests. In the autumn the fallen leaves of trees and bushes should be removed. This can be done by stretching out a plastic net. If frost threatens, sensitive exotic plants should be protected. They can be placed in basins in the house for the cold season. In winter in particular, make sure they have sufficient water. A pond should never freeze through to the bottom. That does not hurt the water plants, as the native species resist frost in nature, but it can be fatal to animals. Salamanders, frogs and fish that dive to the bottom of the pond have no chance if thick ice builds up. A covering of ice does no harm if there is enough water under it. Ice-free systems are useful only in very shallow ponds. But a covering of ice should never be walked on. The footsteps disturb the sleeping animals.

Around the Water Garden

The care of the surrounding areas depends on the kind of plants. Lawns bordering on the lawn get their regular mowing. A flower meadow is mowed only once in summer and once in autumn. Flower beds with larkspurs, purple loosestrife, phlox, and the like need the proper care, cutting back in the fall and fertilizing, such as with compost, in the spring. For trees like willows and alders, pruning according to their type suffices. Only pollard willows need to be trimmed radically every year.

Raising Pollard Willows

Willow trees bear trimming very well. Their great ability to put out shoots has made them valuable, useful trees for hundreds of years. In fact, pollard willows are sources of materials for wickerwork. Every winter they are cut back radically to short stumps. Afterward, they put out yard-long shoots. These elastic willow withes are ideal for woven work such as fences, arbors, and shore reinforcement. Cutting the shoots regularly does not hurt the trees. Instead, it results in an ever more luxuriant head growth. Best suited for use as pollard willows are types that form trunks. The yellow-wood basket willow (*Salix viminalis*) is best, but the white willow (*Salix alba*) and other types also grow usable shoots. Growing them is very simple. At first, a young tree is planted. It is allowed to grow to the desired trunk height. As soon as it has reached that, it is pollarded. After being cut, it puts out several shoots from the cut place. These are cut off in the next winter. Only short stumps remain. Young shoots grow out of each of these stumps. In this way, a typical willow head develops. Such a tree has enough room, and does well by a garden pond. Of course it must be trimmed regularly; otherwise it grows wild and forms a big natural crown. Young trees can be grown easily from cuttings. You need young shoots (such as from a nice old willow tree) that you cut in winter; shorten them to the right length and stick them in pots of moist sand. In the following summer these shoots will grow roots. You can plant the healthy young trees in the garden that autumn.

Planting water plants can be done at any time during the season by using pots. Water lilies need a nutritious substratum.

Preventing the Spread of Prolific Species

Many unwanted plants propagate by themselves. Bärenklau, a.k.a. Hercules Perennial, is particularly vigorous. Umbelliferae (a large family of fragrant or aromatic flowering plants) may be prevented from sowing by removing the seed cones before they mature. The leaves of this wild nettle plant actually contain a poison, which when touched can cause nasty blisters. However, it only acts on sunny days.

Increasing Water and Shore Plants

Water lilies, swamp iris, calamus, and other flowers and grasses that grow on dry land, like phlox, asters or purple loosestrife can be increased most simply and quickly by dividing. Only rooted branches of healthy mother plants are taken, or the entire bushes are dug out and separated into clumps. These "young plants" soon form thick stands again after planting. The best time for dividing is either before the spring growth or after drawing back in autumn. But many plants can also spread from seeds. Healthy seeds that will germinate, and are handled the right way, are needed. Seeding, of course, brings a lot of new plants. In general, it takes longer than dividing. Trees like willows often root by themselves when some twigs break off and are left on the ground. This vitality can be used deliberately to increase them (as in pollard willows). More plants can also be grown from shoots, such as forsythia, poplar, flowering currants, privet, etc.

Differently from potted plants, water lilies can spread in the substratum unhindered. Such clumps are suitable for dividing and increasing; strong root rhizomes are detached.

RENEWING PONDS
Renewing the Pond

Cleaning Out and Recreating Water Gardens

A body of water with a foil lining normally lasts more than fifteen years if it was laid out right. Sometimes, though, a renewal is due, such as if too much soil was filled in and the plants grew too much, or if the water dries up.

Most mistakes are made when building a pond by making shores too steep, filling in nutrient-rich substrata or planting too much. Steep slopes are easily eroded. Thus the foil is left unprotected, so that it is more exposed to the weather. Although special pond foils can stand more or less UV light, they are attacked by it over time. A shielding layer of sand or gravel protects them not only from weather, but also from being walked on or damaged by tools. A covering of soil would be just as effective. But it does not do the water good, as the nutrients in it favor algae buildup and too-luxuriant plant growth. In time the pond is covered with slime. Inert gases are formed. The water deteriorates into an unpleasant scum for lack of oxygen. Then no chemical means or healing methods help any more, but only basic changes. In particular, the wild vegetation has to be decreased and the mud partially dug out.

Above: The strongly rooted shore plants are hard to dig out. Damage to the foil usually cannot be avoided.

Right: Water plants can be planted in flowerpots. There they stay within limits.

Above: By planting them in pots or cages, strong plants develop but the gravel and water areas stay free.

Left: Water lilies should be put in big enough pots. In such pots they have enough root room for a long time.

Above: During the clearing, watch out for animals who hide in the mud. Such actions should be avoided when no nutrient-rich soil is poured into the pond, or just some in small piles.

Left center: Fish and other pond animals can survive the clearing in water basins prepared for them. Meanwhile the water is removed by a powerful pump.

Right center: The soil on the bottom of the pond also allows shallow-water plants to grow into the deep-water zone. During clearing, water lilies and buttercups must be carefully separated.

Right: The nutritious mud is finally composted. With every load, think of withdrawn animals. Some of the mud can be used as a substratum in plant containers.

Upper left: The fleece and the padding layer are still useful. They can, without change, serve as the base for the new pond. The old foil was taken to the landfill.

Upper right: Some plants are retained, as are the gravel and technical devices, as long as they still work and meet safety standards. The water lilies get only a little substratum after replanting.

Center: Before the new structuring, of course changes are possible. Too-steep banks can be cut down or new bays can be dug. Above all, mistaken or unfavorable places should be changed. In the new layout it is important to cover the foil entirely with sand or gravel, so it vanishes completely.

Left: At steep places, large gravel or even angular stones can be used to hide the foil. Plants are placed in the water area deliberately, either in pots or small basins. The water surface should always look big and not get grown up again— unless the pond is to be a clearing basin. Only when the desired water level is reached do the edges of the foil get trimmed. If necessary, underfilling can be done in places. Finally the whole edge seam vanishes under a spreading of gravel.

ALL-YEAR WORK SCHEDULE
Water Gardens as the Seasons Change

Upper left: Water lilies can live indefinitely in a concrete ring or grid basket. After planting, they send their leaves up from the rootstock to the surface of the water.

Upper right: A rain barrel sunk in the ground near the pond is a suitable filter. It is necessary to remove it to lay the foil.

Above: For masonry (such as in a swimming pool) or gapless setting of stones (as in a brook), concrete or mortar is used. It can be mixed dry in a wheelbarrow.

Right: Paving stones have proved themselves as flowerbed edges. They can be dug into the ground in any shapes and—as here—used as a decorative border for a foil pond.

In the winter, a layer of ice
does not damage the garden
pond. The fish can descend
into the deep, frost-free
water and rest on the
bottom. They must not be
disturbed, of course. Only
in a shallow pond is frost
protection or evacuation
necessary.

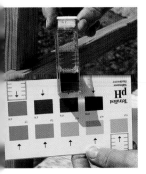

pH Value

This chemical concept is the Latin abbreviation for *potential hydrogenii* and means as much as the potency of the hydrogen. The pH value is a measurement of the acidic degree of a substance. The acidic effect is created by positively charged atoms of hydrogen and negatively charged atoms of oxygen. The pH value indicates the relationship. The values extend from 0 to 14; 0 is extremely acidic, 14 is extremely alkaline (basic). At 7 the relationship is balanced or neutral. Most garden soils are neutral or slightly alkaline, and thus bearable for almost all plants. Only a few definite soils have a sour (such as turf) or alkaline effect (such as chalk marl). They can be neutralized by adding chalk or turf.

pH Value:	1	2	3	5	7	9	11	12	14
	extremely sour		strongly sour		neutral		strongly alkaline		extremely alkaline

Tips:

To compare some values:

Vinegar has a pH value of 3.

Water is in the neutral area around 7.

Turf is sour at 4-5.

Calcium fertilizer is alkaline (ca. 8).

Garden compost has a value between 6.5 and 8.

Common Indicator Plants

Type	Property
Coltsfoot	high chalk content
Nettle	humus soil high nitrogen content
Dandelion	nutrient-rich lime soil
Thistle	nutrient-rich lime soil
Chickweed	humus soil, high nutrient content
Galinsoga	humus soil, high nutrient content

Coltsfoot on a chalk soil.

Prices (approximate) for Concrete and Natural Stone per Square Meter (selection)

Cinder block (normal size)	30 Euro = $41.76
Granite stone (8 x 11 cm)	40 Euro = $55.69
Porphyry (cubes, 8 x 11 cm)	50 Euro = $69.58
Concrete block (H-shape)	16 Euro = $22.25
Concrete plate (walkway, 50 x 50 cm)	16 Euro = $22.25
Concrete plate (smooth, pinkish, 40 x 40 cm)	40 Euro = $55.69
Washed concrete plate (40 x 40 cm)	20 Euro = $27.81
Quartzite plate	50 Euro = $69.58
Chalk paving stone	35 Euro = $48.67
Porphyry plate (broken pieces)	16 Euro = $22.25

The prices depend on the amount purchased.

Prices per ton represent some 5 square meters.

(for example, 1 ton of granite stone at 180 Euro = 5 square meters of paving surface at 36 Euro).

Plus shipping and crane costs for unloading, plus value-added tax.

The costs for laying depend on the material, according to substructure and suitability of the paving stones or plates for being worked.

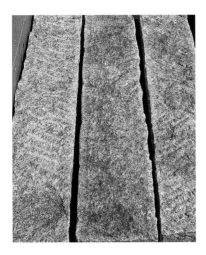

Law pavement (concrete)

Concrete wall, built with the help of a scaling.

Small stone pavement (chalk)

Gravel

Flowering Plants (selection)

Species	Height	Color	Blooms	Location
Columbine: *Aquilegia vulgaris*	50 cm	blue	May-June	partial shade
Bearded Iris: *Iris barbata*	70 cm	varied	May-June	sunny
Saxifrage: *Bergenia sp.*	30 cm	pink	April-May	sunny, shady
Cornflower: *Centaurea montana*	50 cm	blue	May-August	sunny, shady
Maltese Cross: *Lychnis chalcedonica*	70 cm	red	June-July	sunny
Christmas Rose: *Helleborus niger*	30 cm	white, violet	Dec.-March	sunny, shady
Spiderwort: *Tradescantia andersoniana*	50 cm	blue	July-Sept.	sunny, shady
Monkshood: *Aconitum napellus*	130 cm	blue	July-Sept.	sunny, shady
Sedum: *Sedum telephium*	50 cm	red	Sept.-Oct.	sunny
Primrose: *Primula vulgaris*	20 cm	varied	March-April	sunny, shady
Leopard's Bane: *Doronicum caucasicum*	40 cm	yellow	April-May	sunny
Garden Loosestrife: *Lysimachia punctata*	60 cm	yellow	June-Aug.	sunny, shady
Fall Anemone: *Anemone hupehensis*	100 cm	red, white	August-Oct.	partial shade
New England and New York Aster: *Aster novae-angliae and novi-belgii*	130 cm	red, blue	Sept.-Oct.	sunny
Bee Balm: *Monarda sp.*	100 cm	red	July-Sept.	sunny, shady
Catmint: *Nepeta x faassenii*	50 cm	blue	May-Oct.	sunny
Aster: *Aster dumosus*	40cm	pink, blue	August-Oct.	sunny
Blanket Flower: *Gaillardia sp.*	50 cm	yellow-red	June-Sept.	sunny
Ligularia: *Ligularia sp.*	120 cm	yellow	August-Sept.	partial shade

Above: Purple cornflower *(Echinacea purpurea)*

Below: Larkspur *(Delphinium sp.)*

Flowering plants (selection)

Species	Height	Color	Blooms	Location
Lupine: *Lupinus sp.*	80 cm	varied	July-Aug.	sunny, shady
Tickseed: *Coreopsis verticillata*	60 cm	yellow	July-Aug.	sunny, shady
Peony: *Paeonia officinalis*	80 cm	red	April-June	sunny-shady
Astilbe: *Astilbe sp.*	100 cm	pink, white	July-Aug.	sunny, shady
Purple Coneflower: *Echinacea purpurea*	100 cm	red	July-Sept.	sunny
Larkspur: *Delphinium sp.*	120 cm	blue	June-July	sunny
Salvia: *Salvia nemorosa*	30 cm	blue	June-July	sunny
Gold Yarrow: *Achillea filipendula*	120 cm	yellow	June-Aug.	full sun
Milfoil Yarrow: *Achuillea millefolia*	60 cm	white, red	June-Sept.	full sun
Chrysanthemum: *Chrysanthemum maximum*	80 cm	white	July-Sept.	sunny
Sneezeweed: *Helenium sp.*	100-150 cm	yellow, brown	July-Oct.	sunny
Coneflower: *Rudbeckia sullivantii*	70 cm	yellow	Aug.-Oct.	sunny
Red Valerian: *Centranthus rubber*	60 cm	red	June-Aug.	sunny
Phlox: *Phlox paniculata*	100 cm	varied	June-Sept.	sunny
Thin-Leaf Sunflower: *Helianthus decapetalus*	120 cm	yellow	Aug.-Sept.	sunny
Geranium: *Geranium sp.*	50 cm	pink	June-Aug.	sunny, shady
Day Lily: *Hemerocallis sp.*	80 cm	yellow, red	June-July	sunny, shady
Oriental Poppy: *Papaver orientale*	70 cm	red	May-June	sunny
Goat's-Beard: *Aruncus dioicus*	150 cm	white	June-July	shady

Above: Oxlip *(Primula elatior)*

Below: Oxeye Daisy *(Chrysanthemum sp.)*

Appendix

You will often find water gardens in nearby botanical gardens, displays of garden shops, state garden shows, and other places open to the public. In addition, taking a look over the fence into a garden development is worth doing, as is talking with garden owners who have already put in a pond.

Photo Credits

The front cover photo was taken in the display flower garden of Weihenstephan (in the orchard).

Other Photo Sources of Gardens Worth Seeing:

p. 6, Eckert Professional Training Center, Regenstauf
p. 7 & p. 33 top, County Training Garden, Regenstauf
p. 9, County Training Garden, Walderbach on the Regen (there is also a water-lily grower in the town).
p. 11, Dehner Family Display in Rain on the Lech.
p. 13, p. 15, & p. 61, Botanical Gardens, Augsburg
p. 21, Kneipp Center, Koenigswiesen, Regensburg
p. 33 below, Botanical Gardens, Freiburg
p. 97, p. 98, & p. 110, Botanical Gardens, Regensburg]

Projects were built by or with the help of:

Swimming pool: Bengler-Hillenmayer family, Burglengenfeld, p. 66
Bathing pool: Nutt family, Regenstauf, p. 86
Plastic basin: Himmelhuber family, Leonberg, p. 94
Water steps: Engel family, Eilsbrunn, p. 44
Granite fountain: Wagner-Ruell family, Nuernberg, p. 48
Brook course: Neumann family, Wenzenbach, p. 112
Foil pond: Frank family, Burgweinting, p. 29
Concrete cistern: Peter Beer, Wackersdorf, p. 106
Pond renewal: Kiener family, Leonberg, among others, p. 145

The Design Drawings for the Swimming Pool were drawn by Franz Hillenmayer, p. 69

The Pond Model of a wading pool is by Manfred Nutt, p. 10

Special thanks to the garden owners and collaborators for the change to take photographs, likewise to the garden-building firm of Nicolai and Spitzer, who built the brook, among other things, and the Wagner firm of Burglengenfeld with its excavator, responsible for, among others, the excavation and material for the swimming pool.

BIBLIOGRAPHY

In any case, obtaining specialist books and periodicals is worth doing. The givers of special advice help to avoid errors and keep costs down. The publishers also answer readers' special questions at no charge.

Select Bibliography

Barth, Ursula, *Teiche und Badeteiche*, Munich 2000

Bastian, Hans W., *Selbst Regenwasser-Nutzsysteme anlagen*, 7th ed., Munich 1997

Bauch-Troschke, Zita, *Brunnen, Wasserbecken und Wasserspiele*, Munich 2000

Bund deutsche Baumschulen (ed.), *Handbuch des Wassers und des Wasserrandes*, Berlin 1999

Clark, Ronald, *Garten-Reisefuehrer*, Munich 2003

Dobler, Anna & Wolfgang Fleischer, *Schwimmteiche*, Vienna 1999

Hecker, Frank & Kathrin, *Treffpunkt Teich und Tuempel*, 2003

Helberg, Thomas, *Gartenteiche*, 2nd ed., Stuttgart 2003

Hilgenstock/Witt, *Das Naturgarten-Baubuch*, Munich 2003

Himmelhuber, Peter, *Selbst Brunnen, Wasserspiele und Baeche bauen*, Stuttgart 2002

Hobhouse, Penelope & Patrick Taylor, *Gaerten in Europe*, Stuttgart 1992

Howcroft, Heidi, *Brunnen*, Munich 2001

Jorek, Norbert, *Beispielhafte Gartenteiche*, 15th ed., Munich 2003

Love, Gilly, *Wasser im Garten*, Munich 2002

Neuenschwander, Eduard, *Schwimmteiche*, Stuttgart 2000

Schmidt, Loki, *Die Botanischen Gaerten in Deutschland*, Hamburg 1997

Teichfischer, Bernhard, *Koi in den schoensten Wassergaerten*, Ettlingen 2001

Wachter, Karl, *Seerosen*, Stuttgart 1998

The author recommends Ronald Clark's *Gartenreisefuehrer* (Garden Guide) as a guide for visiting private and public gardens.

Selected Organizations

Zentralverband Gartenbau e.V. (ZVG)
Godesberger Allee 142-148, 53144 Bonn
Tel. 0228-81002-0
www.g-net.de

Bund deutscher Baumschulen e.V. (BdB)
Bismarckstrasse 49, 25402 Pinneberg
Tel. 04101-2039-0
www.bund-deutscher-baumschulen.de

Bund deutscher Staudengaertner
Godesberger Allee 142-148, 53175 Bonn
Tel. 0228-8100251
www.stauden.de

Bund fuer Umwelt und Naturschutz e.V. (BUND)
Am Koellnischen Park 1, 10179 Berlin
Tel. 0228-40097-0
www.bund-berlin.de

Verband Oesterreichischer Schwimmteichbauer
Aichbergstrasse 48, 4600 Vienna, Austria
Tel. 0043-7242-66692
www.schwimmteich.co.at

INDEX

MORE SCHIFFER TITLES

www.schifferbooks.com

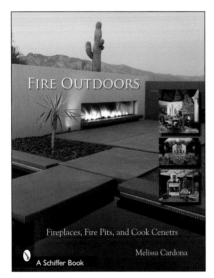

Fire Outdoors: Fireplaces, Fire Pits, & Cook Centers. Tina Skinner & Melissa Cardona. From warm weather climates to properties built on permafrost, homeowners everywhere are discovering anew the allure of fire outdoors. With zoning laws, resources, and proximity often limiting the open bonfire enjoyed by our ancestors, fire is being tamed in a variety of attractive ways by creative landscape architects, designers, builders, and manufacturers. Today's outdoor fires radiate warmth for chilly evenings, add an attractive glow to gathered faces, form focal centers for outdoor gatherings, and provide a means of food preparation al fresco.

This book presents a wide variety of ideas of outdoor fireplaces, fire pits, and cook centers. Manufactured outdoor hearth products and custom handmade masterpieces address a huge array of styles to satisfy a broad range of tastes and budgets. A selection of outdoor cook centers is also included, complete with wood burning pizza ovens. Over 200 images of designs by professional landscape architects, contractors, custom homebuilders, kitchen designers, and hearth product manufacturers were compiled to provide inspiration and present the most complete book on the subject ever published.

Size: 8 1/2" x 11" • 225 color photos • 144 pp.
ISBN: 0-7643-2397-0 • soft cover • $19.95

Creating Ponds, Brooks, and Pools: Water in the Garden. Ulrich Timm. Water forms the soul of a garden. A quiet pond, a babbling brook, or a dramatic pool can make a garden unique. To achieve such beauty, however, requires careful planning and design. Using over 150 brilliant color photographs, this splendid and inspiring book presents the variety of possibilities for using water in the garden. The informative and enjoyable text provides helpful planning details, including advice on waterproofing, the shore formation, attractive plantings, even fish. Planning and building any kind of water garden is not only fun, it greatly enriches the joy that is found in one's own backyard garden.

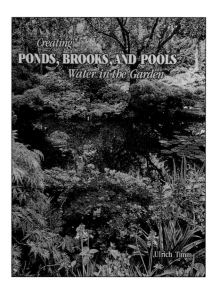

Size: 8 1/2" x 11" • Over 150 color photos • 160 pp.
ISBN: 0-7643-0915-3 • hard cover • $29.95

Creative Patios. Tina Skinner. This collection of beautiful photographs showcases the artistry of those who sculpt outdoor living environments with solid rock, impressed and tinted concrete, and brick in many forms. You will be both inspired and informed. This practical guidebook will help you choose a patio style suitable for your home, learn to speak your contractor's language, pick a plan that fits your budget and style, furnish and organize outdoor areas for entertaining or intimate family dining, create containers and border areas for dynamic gardens and landscaping displays, and develop outdoor sanctuaries with artfully placed planter boxes, shrubs, and privacy screens. There are also step-by-step instructions for the successful installation of your own paver patio!

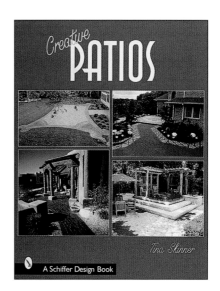

Size: 8 1/2" x 11" • 310 photos • Resource Guide • 192 pp.
ISBN: 0-7643-1278-2 • soft cover • $29.95

Natural Swimming Pools: Inspiration for Harmony with Nature. Michael Littlewood FLI, FSGD. Natural swimming pools rely on the correct balance of living plants and micro-organisms to clean and purify the water. They are easy and less costly to maintain than chemical pools. Chlorine and other common pool chemicals that are hazardous to human health are not used. Natural pools are safe places for children to play and birds to drink, and are a dramatic example of ecological design, combining the natural and man-made worlds while creating beauty. These pools offer enjoyment not only in the warm months, but during winter, when they can be used for ice skating.

Often the focal point of a garden, a natural swimming pool blends into the environment, flowing into the surroundings with plants and rocks. It reflects the changing seasons and enhances the environment naturally.

This book is a necessary resource for people who consider a natural swimming pool. It shows how the natural system works to provide environmental, health, and safety benefits. Drawings, diagrams, and charts help explain their planning, design, biology, materials, construction, planting, and maintenance.

Over 300 beautiful color photographs of natural pools will inspire your own water garden, where you can swim in harmony with nature.

Size: 8 1/2" x 11" • 300+ color photos • Resource Guide • 256 pp. ISBN: 0-7643-2183-8 • hard cover • $49.95

Schiffer books may be ordered from your local bookstore, or they may be ordered directly from the publisher by writing to:

Schiffer Publishing, Ltd.
4880 Lower Valley Road
Atglen PA 19310
(610) 593-1777; Fax (610) 593-2002
E-mail: Info@schifferbooks.com

Please visit our web site catalog at: www.schifferbooks.com or write for a free catalog. Please include $5.00 for shipping and handling for the first two books and $2.00 for each additional book. Full-price orders over $150 are shipped free in the U.S.

Printed in China

VERMONT STATE COLLEGES

0 0003 0846164 9

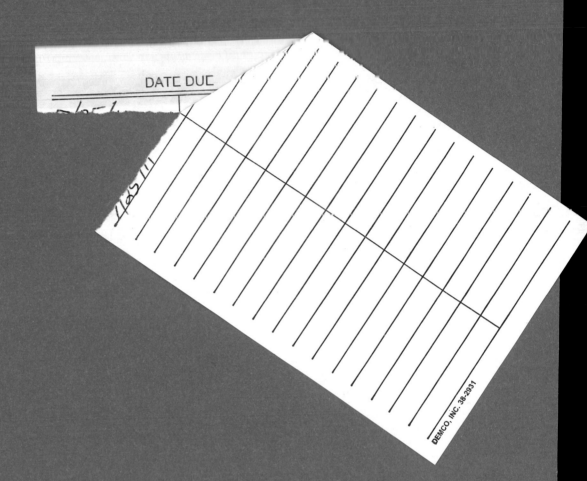

DEMCO, INC. 38-2931

DATE DUE

HARTNESS LIBRARY SYSTEM
Vermont Technical College/CCV
Randolph Center, VT 05061

DISCARD